INTEGRATING MATHEMATICS, SCIENCE, AND TECHNOLOGY

A Skill-Building Approach

DIANA MASON

University of North Texas

KATHLEEN CAGE MITTAG

The University of Texas at San Antonio

SHARON E. TAYLOR

Georgia Southern University

Boston   New York   San Francisco
Mexico City   Montreal   Toronto   London   Madrid   Munich   Paris
Hong Kong   Singapore   Tokyo   Cape Town   Sydney

*To all those who have gone before us, we give you our thanks;
to those who are still supporting us emotionally and academically,
we are gratefully indebted.*

Series Editor: *Traci Mueller*
Editorial Assistant: *Erica Tromblay*
Senior Marketing Manager: *Elizabeth Fogarty*
Editorial-Production Service: *Omegatype Typography, Inc.*
Manufacturing Buyer: *Andrew Turso*
Composition and Prepress Buyer: *Linda Cox*
Cover Administrator: *Kristina Mose-Libon*
Electronic Composition: *Omegatype Typography, Inc.*

For related titles and support materials, visit our online catalogue at www.ablongman.com.

Library of Congress Cataloging-in-Publication Data
Mason, Diana J.
    Integrating mathematics, science, and technology : a skill-building approach / Diana
Mason, Kathleen Cage Mittag, Sharon E. Taylor.
        p. cm.
    Includes bibliographical references.
    ISBN 0-205-34994-3 (alk. paper)
        1. Science—Study and teaching (Middle school)—United States.   2. Mathematics—Study
and teaching (Middle school)—United States.   3. Science—Study and teaching
(Secondary)—United States.   4. Mathematics—Study and teaching (Secondary)—United
States.   I. Mittag, Kathleen Cage.   II. Taylor, Sharon E.   III. Title.

Q183.3.A1 M37 2003
507'.1'273—dc21

                                                                2002075798

Contents

Acknowledgments

This project could not have been completed without the support and careful editing of Professor Paul Westmeyer. His assistance provided a platform that guided and nurtured this project from its inception.

We are also greatly indebted to Violetta Lien and Carmen Fies for their contributions to this integrated textbook. Both of these science education specialists were able to contribute chapters beyond the expertise of the primary authors. Specifically, Dr. Lien wrote the chapters on the atmosphere and light, and Carmen Fies contributed the chapter on electricity.

Much of the success of this work is based on the dedication of our colleagues, students, and workshop attendees, who tested the materials, gave advice and support, and encouraged us to continue. We thank them for their feedback and assistance.

We also wish to thank the following reviewers: Belinda Anderson, Lambuth University; Patrick Casey, St. Bonaventure University; and William Hessmiller, Med Com Technologies.

Introduction

You cannot hope to build a better world without improving the individuals. To that end, each of us must work for our own improvement and, at the same time, share a general responsibility for all humanity, our particular duty being to aid those to whom we think we can be most useful.
—Marie Curie

BACKGROUND

The science and mathematics education community has spent the last decade talking about change and integration across the curriculum. Many communities have adopted both the National Science Education Standards (NSES) and those reported by the National Council of Teachers of Mathematics (NCTM), yet educators have failed to develop instructional materials that do more than give lip service to the integration of science and mathematics. Without a question, there is natural integration of these two disciplines. Mathematics is the language used by scientists to communicate to others across the globe. This communication occurs with minimum (if any) delay, thanks to the many advances in technology.

This laboratory-based book integrates mathematics, science, and technology. Its inception was the result of need. While teaching college students courses in mathematics and science; conducting in-service staff development sessions; and presenting conference workshops integrating mathematics, science, and technology, the authors noticed deficiencies in available materials as well as student and in-service teacher needs for more content knowledge. None of the available activities found seemed truly integrated. The mathematics teachers expressed a need for more examples of application problems appropriate for the classroom, and the science teachers wanted more knowledge on how to integrate technology into their curriculum. Also, attempting to find one textbook to fit these needs proved futile, and each author realized our lack of expertise to teach outside of our respective fields. However, we knew that if we combined our efforts, we could develop a book based on sound pedagogy that delivered foundational content in mathematics and science with the use of technology. Hence the conception of this guided-inquiry laboratory and skill-building book.

Each activity begins as a traditional science laboratory, then carefully intertwines mathematics and technology portions into laboratory activities in such a way that all three are truly integrated. Scientific concepts from physics, earth science, chemistry, biology, and the related mathematics are woven together along with the appropriate technology. Appropriate standards from science and mathematics as well as meaningful technology are presented. After the explanation of the concepts, the procedure is outlined, followed by student laboratory datasheets. Extensions conclude the activities, giving students opportunities to connect the laboratory experiences to practical, real-world applications. Each chapter is designed to take approximately three hours to complete with university students. High school and middle school teachers should change this timeline accordingly.

RESEARCH

Integration of Mathematics and Science

This book incorporates current research findings concerning integrated mathematics and science curricula, technology, pedagogy, and teacher professional development. In *Integrated Mathematics and Science Curricula,* Lederman and Niess (1998) discussed the methodological differences between mathematics and science when they wrote, "Whereas science seeks consistency with the natural/external world through empirical evidence, mathematics seeks consistency within its internal system through logical deduction" (p. 281). Several sources such as the National Council of Teachers of Mathematics' *Principles and Standards for School Mathematics* (2000) and *Science for All Americans* (American Association for the Advancement of Science, 1989) agree that both science and mathematics seek to find and make sense of patterns. We have incorporated science and mathematics foci equally in this instructional guide. Berlin (1991) found that this was seldom done, and other current projects support the fact that science is the focus of integrated science and mathematics programs (Hedgepeth, 1995; Lehman & Kandl, 1995; Roth & Bowen, 1994). Watanabe and Huntley (1998) stressed the need for classroom instruction to emphasize the connections between mathematics and science. Also, many sources have recommended the integration of mathematics and science (AAAS, 1989; Darling-Hammond & Ball, 1999; NCTM, 1989, 1991, 1995; National Research Council, 1996a, 1996b; Roth, 1992).

Technology

Technology use is of paramount importance to this book. The graphing calculator and other data collection and processing devices are used frequently. Many research results indicate the benefits of the calculator as a tool in the classroom (Campbell & Stewart, 1993; Carlson, 1996; Dunham, 1993, 1996; Harvey, Waits, & Demana, 1995; Hembree & Dessart, 1986; Quesada, 1994; Smith, 1997). Teachers not only have to train their students in the content area, but now also have to train students on how to use the tools available to the classroom (Demana & Waits, 1990; Dunham & Dick, 1994; Fey & Good, 1985). Pang and Good (2000, p. 78) list the following benefits of technology use in integrated mathematics and science classrooms:

1. Facilitates collaboration among users
2. Provides the contextualized nature of problem solving
3. Reduces limits on instructional time
4. Allows students to apply their knowledge to a practical task

Pedagogy

The basic pedagogy used in this book is that of skill development and guided inquiry supported by the appropriate historical background in science and mathematics—in other words, how scientific thought came into being behind a strong mathematical foundation. This text is written for scientists and mathematicians who desire a technical reference to prepare future science and mathematics teachers or to cross-train science and mathematics teachers from various backgrounds. Inquiry learning is supported by numerous sources and appears in both the NCTM *Standards* document and the NSES *Standards* document. "Hands-on, minds-on" is a popular teaching strategy. The teaching strategy of using activity-based learning, collaborative groupings, and classroom exercises mirrors the ACE cycle (activities, class discussion, and exercises) advocated by Asiala et al. (1996). Woods and Thompson (1980) and Rudolph and Preston (1995) stressed the importance of "modeling," in which participants or students actually do the activities during workshops or classes.

Professional Development

Teacher training is a significant factor determining student achievement (Ferguson, 1991; Greenwald, Hedges, & Laine, 1996). Darling-Hammond (1992) found that 48 percent of high school students taking physical science were taught by out-of-field teachers. In 1994 Darling-Hammond and Ball (1999) found that only 53 percent of U.S. mathematics teachers have both a license and a major in their field. They stated that "in short, many U.S. teachers enter the profession with inadequate preparation, and few have opportunities to enhance their knowledge and skills over the course of their careers" (1999, p. 11). Elementary teachers do not feel qualified or adequately prepared to teach science (George et al., 1996). Underhill, Abdi, and Peters (1994) drew the following conclusions from studying the Virginia State Systemic Initiative: "The planning team believes that for mathematics and science teachers to meet the challenge to integrate mathematics and science in their instruction, they need support, retraining, and professional empowerment to help them bring about necessary changes" (p. 26).

Rarely is this type of directed teaching available to the undergraduate teacher education major. The fear and anxiety of teaching science and mathematics have two components: (1) the teachers' own background experiences are limited (few elementary teachers have had a college chemistry or physics course) and (2) these courses in college are primarily lecture courses, not hands-on or interactive. The majority of educators will teach as they were taught. Because inquiry and problem-solving instruction are not generally part of their experience, this important combination of teaching strategies seldom occurs. The teachers are being asked to use inquiry and problem-solving strategies in their own instructional situations with no prior experience, and there is more pressure on teachers to use a constructivist approach to teaching.

Many in-service teachers (one of our major targeted audiences) were never exposed to or trained to use this pedagogy; therefore, staff-development workshops need to be modeled using a constructivist approach for teachers to meet the expectations of the science and mathematics reform movements (Bellanca, 1995; Sparks, 1995).

FEATURES OF THE BOOK

This book is arranged so that it can be used in the following applications:

1. As an undergraduate (mathematics or science) text for teacher education courses
2. As a graduate teacher education text for a course on integrated mathematics, science, and technology
3. As a supplemental text by middle and high school mathematics and science teachers
4. As a staff development program for elementary to secondary level in-service teachers

The best feature of this book is that it is usable by mathematics and science teachers, not limited to one population or the other. Although there are a few science–mathematics educational-technology integrated activities, they are usually geared either for science teachers or for mathematics teachers only. Because this book has been written by science and mathematics educators, it is easily understood by both science and mathematics teachers. The integration of technology is another unique feature. Some science activity books have integrated technology such as data collection devices and graphing calculators with very little mathematical reference. Mathematics texts and supplemental activity books regularly include graphing calculator keystroke activities, but with no science background provided. The integration of mathematics, science, and technology is truly unique. Chapter One includes instructions on how to use a graphing calculator.

Each chapter begins with an introduction and then presents the science and mathematics concepts to be included. The concepts to be included are then expanded and followed by one or more investigations. The investigations include a purpose, equipment and materials needed, and directions for the procedure. Student worksheets are also included with wrap-up questions involving higher-order thinking skills and problem-solving challenges.

REFERENCES

American Association for the Advancement of Science (AAAS). (1989). *Science for all Americans: Project 2061*. Washington, DC: Author.

Asiala, M., Brown, A., DeVries, D. J., Dubinsky, E., Mathews, D., & Thomas, K. (1996). A framework for research and curriculum development in undergraduate mathematics education. *CBMS Issues in Mathematics Education, 6,* 1–32.

Bellanca, J. (1995). *Designing professional development for change: A systematic approach.* Arlington Heights, IL: IRI/Skylight Training and Publishing.

Berlin, D. F. (1991). A bibliography of integrated science and mathematics teaching and learning literature. *School Science and Mathematics Association Topics for Teacher Series* (No. 6). Bowling Green, OH: School Science and Mathematics Association.

Campbell, P., & Stewart, E. L. (1993). Calculators and computers. In R. Jensen, *Early Childhood Mathematics, NCTM Research Interpretation Project* (pp. 251–268). New York: Macmillan.

Carlson, M. P. (1996). A successful transition to a calculator integrated college algebra curriculum: Clues, surveys, and trends. In *Proceedings of the Seventh Annual International Conference on Technology in Collegiate Mathematics* (pp. 73–77). Reading, MA: Addison Wesley.

Darling-Hammond, L. (1992). Teaching and knowledge: Policy issues posed by alternative certification of teachers. *Peabody Journal of Education, 67,* 123–154.

Darling-Hammond, L., & Ball, D. L. (1999). *Teaching for High Standards: What Policymakers Need to Know and Be Able to Do.* Consortium for Policy Research in Education Joint Report Series, co-published with the National Commission on Teaching and America's Future. New York: Teacher's College, Columbia University.

Demana, F., & Waits, B. K. (1990). Implementing the standards: The role of technology in teaching mathematics. *Mathematics Teacher, 83,* 27–31.

Dunham, P. H. (1993). Does using calculators work? The jury is almost in. *UME Trends, 5*(2), 8–9.

Dunham, P. H. (1996). Looking for trends: What's new in graphing calculator research? In *Proceedings of the Eighth Annual International Conference on Technology in Collegiate Mathematics* (pp. 120–124). Reading, MA: Addison Wesley.

Dunham, P. H., & Dick, T. P. (1994). Research on graphing calculators. *Mathematics Teacher, 87,* 440–445.

Ferguson, R. (1991). Paying for public education: New evidence on how and why money matters. *Harvard Journal of Legislation, 28,* 465–498.

Fey, J. T., & Good, R. A. (1985). Rethinking the sequence and priorities of high school mathematics curricula. In C. R. Hirsch & J. Zweng, *The Secondary School Mathematics Curriculum, 1985 Yearbook* (pp. 43–52). Reston, VA: National Council of Teachers of Mathematics.

George, M. D., Brass, S., de los Santos, A. G., Denton, D. D., Gerber, P., Lindquist, M. M., Rosser, J. M., Sanchez, D. A., & Meyers, C. (1996). *Shaping the future: New expectations for undergraduate education in science, mathematics, engineering, and technology* (NSF 96-139). Arlington, VA: Directorate for Education and Human Resources, National Science Foundation.

Greenwald, R., Hedges, L. V., & Laine, R. D. (1996). The effect of school resources on student achievement. *Review of Educational Research, 66,* 361–396.

Harvey, J. G., Waits, B. K., & Demana, F. D. (1995). The influence of technology on the teaching and learning of algebra. *Journal of Mathematical Behavior, 14,* 75–109.

Hedgepeth, D. J. (1995). Measuring the nutrient tolerance of algae. *School Science and Mathematics, 95*(2), 102–107.

Hembree, R., & Dessart, D. J. (1986). Effects of hand-held calculators in precollege mathematics education: A meta-analysis. *Journal for Research in Mathematics Education, 17,* 83–89.

Lederman, N. G., & Niess, M. L. (1998). 5 apples + 4 oranges =? *School Science and Mathematics, 98*(6), 281–284.

Lehman, J. R., & Kandl, T. M. (1995). Popcorn investigations for integrating mathematics, science and technology. *School Science and Mathematics, 95*(61), 46–49.

National Academy of Science (NAS). (1996). *National science education standards.* Washington, DC: National Academy Press.

National Council of Teachers of Mathematics (NCTM). (1989). *Curriculum and evaluation standards for school mathematics.* Reston, VA: Author.

National Council of Teachers of Mathematics (NCTM). (1991). *Professional standards for teaching mathematics.* Reston, VA: Author.

National Council of Teachers of Mathematics (NCTM) (1995). *Assessment standards for school mathematics.* Reston, VA: Author.

National Council of Teachers of Mathematics (NCTM). (2000). *NCTM Principles and standards for school mathematics.* Reston, VA: Author.

National Research Council (NRC). (1996a). *A report to the nation on the future of mathematics education.* Washington, DC: National Academy Press.

National Research Council (NRC). (1996b). *National science education standards.* Washington, DC: National Academy Press.

Pang, J. S., & Good, R. (2000). A review of the integration of science and mathematics: Implications for further research. *School Science and Mathematics, 100*(2), 73–82.

Quesada, A. R. (1994). On the effects of using graphing calculators in precalculus and calculus, part III. In L. Lum (Ed.), *Proceedings of the Sixth Annual International Conference on Technology in Collegiate Mathematics* (pp. 296–300). Reading, MA: Addison Wesley.

Roth, W. M. (1992). Bridging the gap between school and real life: Toward an integration of science, mathematics, and technology in the context of authentic practice. *School Science and Mathematics, 92*(6), 307–317.

Roth, W. M., & Bowen, G. M. (1994). Mathematization of experience in a grade 8 open-inquiry environment: An introduction to the representational practices of science. *Journal of Research in Science Teaching, 31*(3), 293–318.

Rudolph, S., & Preston, L. (1995). Teaching teachers: The elements of successful workshop design. *The Science Teacher, 62*(6), 30–32.

Smith, B. A. (1997). A meta-analysis of outcomes from the use of calculators in mathematics education. *Dissertation Abstracts International, 58,* 787A.

Sparks, D. (1995). A paradigm shift in professional development. *ERIC Review, 3*(3), 2–4.

Suter, L. (Ed.). (1993). *Indicators of science and mathematics education 1992* (NSF 93-95). Washington, DC: Division of Research, Evaluation, and Dissemination, National Science Foundation.

Underhill, R. G., Abdi, W. W., & Peters, P. F. (1994). The Virginia state systemic initiative: A brief overview of the lead teacher component and a description of the evolving mathematics and science integration outcomes. *School Science and Mathematics, 94*(1), 26–29.

Watanabe, T., & Huntley, M. A. (1998). Connecting mathematics and science in undergraduate teacher education programs: Faculty voices from the Maryland collaborative for teacher preparation. *School Science and Mathematics, 98*(1), 19–25.

Woods, F. H., & Thompson, S. R. (1980). Guidelines for better staff development. *Educational Researcher, 37*(2), 374–378.

	MATHEMATICS CONTENT STANDARDS BY CHAPTER											
	2	3	4	5	6	7	8	9	10	11	12	13
Numbers and Operations												
Understand numbers, ways of representing numbers, relationships among numbers, and number systems	■	■	■									
Understand meanings of operations and how they relate to one another	■	■	■	■	■	■	■					
Compute fluently and make reasonable estimates	■	■	■	■	■	■	■					
Algebra												
Understand patterns, relations, and functions			■	■	■	■	■	■	■	■		
Represent and analyze mathematical situations and structures using algebraic symbols			■	■	■	■	■	■				
Use mathematical models to represent and understand quantitative relationships			■	■	■	■	■	■				
Analyze change in various contexts					■	■	■					
Geometry												
Analyze characteristics and properties of two- and three-dimensional geometric shapes and develop mathematical arguments about geometric relationships											■	
Specify locations and describe spatial relationships using coordinate geometry and other representational systems			■	■	■	■	■		■	■		
Apply transformations and use symmetry to analyze mathematical situations						■					■	
Use visualization, spatial reasoning, and geometric modeling to solve problems											■	
Measurement												
Understand measurable attributes of objects and the units, systems, and processes of measurement	■	■	■	■								
Apply appropriate techniques, tools, and formulas to determine measurements	■	■	■	■	■	■	■	■	■	■	■	■

MATHEMATICS CONTENT STANDARDS BY CHAPTER

	2	3	4	5	6	7	8	9	10	11	12	13
Data Analysis and Probability												
Formulate questions that can be addressed with data and collect, organize, and display relevant data to answer them			■	■	■	■	■	■	■	■		
Select and use appropriate statistical methods to analyze data			■	■	■	■	■	■	■	■		
Develop and evaluate inferences and predictions that are based on data			■	■	■	■	■	■	■	■		
Understand and apply basic concepts of probability							■					
Problem Solving												
Build new mathematical knowledge through problem solving	■	■	■	■	■	■	■	■	■	■	■	■
Solve problems that arise in mathematics and other contexts	■	■	■	■	■	■	■	■	■	■	■	■
Apply and adapt a variety of appropriate strategies to solve problems	■	■	■	■	■	■	■	■	■	■	■	■
Monitor and reflect on the process of mathematical problem solving	■	■	■	■	■	■	■	■	■	■	■	■
Reasoning and Proof												
Recognize reasoning and proof as fundamental aspects of mathematics	■	■										
Make and investigate mathematical conjectures	■	■	■	■	■	■	■	■	■	■	■	■
Develop and evaluate mathematical arguments and proofs	■	■	■									
Select and use various types of reasoning and methods of proof			■	■	■	■	■					
Communication												
Organize and consolidate mathematical thinking through communication	■	■	■	■	■	■	■	■	■	■	■	■
Communicate mathematical thinking coherently and clearly to peers, teachers, and others	■	■	■	■	■	■	■	■	■	■	■	■
Analyze and evaluate the mathematical thinking and strategies of others			■	■	■	■	■					
Use the language of mathematics to express mathematical ideas precisely	■	■	■	■	■	■	■	■	■	■	■	■

MATHEMATICS CONTENT STANDARDS BY CHAPTER

	2	3	4	5	6	7	8	9	10	11	12	13
Connections												
Recognize and use connections among mathematical ideas	■	■	■	■	■	■	■	■	■	■	■	■
Understand how mathematical ideas interconnect and build on one another to produce a coherent whole	■	■	■	■	■	■	■	■	■	■	■	■
Recognize and apply mathematics in contexts outside of mathematics	■	■	■	■	■	■	■	■	■	■	■	■
Representation												
Create and use representations to organize, record, and communicate mathematical ideas	■	■	■	■	■	■	■	■	■	■	■	■
Select, apply, and translate among mathematical representations to solve problems	■	■	■	■	■	■	■	■	■	■	■	■
Use representations to model and interpret physical, social, and mathematical phenomena	■	■	■	■	■	■	■	■	■	■	■	■

SCIENCE CONTENT STANDARDS BY CHAPTER

	2	3	4	5	6	7	8	9	10	11	12	13
Science as Inquiry												
Abilities necessary to do scientific inquiry			■	■	■	■	■	■	■	■		
Understandings about scientific inquiry			■	■	■	■	■	■	■	■		
Physical Science												
Structure of atoms							■					
Structure and properties of matter							■					
Chemical reactions								■				
Motions and forces					■							
Conservation of energy and increase in disorder			■									
Interactions of energy and matter			■									
Life Science												
The cell									■			
Molecular basis of heredity								■				
Biological evolution									■			
Interdependence of organisms								■				
Matter, energy, and organization in living systems									■			
Behavior of organisms									■			

SCIENCE CONTENT STANDARDS BY CHAPTER

	2	3	4	5	6	7	8	9	10	11	12	13
Earth and Space Science												
Energy in the earth system										■		
Geochemical cycles										■		
Origin and evolution of the earth system										■		
Origin and evolution of the universe										■		
Science and Technology												
Abilities of technological design			■	■	■	■	■	■	■	■		
Understand about science and technology	■	■	■	■	■	■	■	■	■	■	■	■
Science in Personal and Social Perspectives												
Personal and community health									■	■		
Population growth								■				
Natural resources										■		
Environmental quality										■		
Natural and human-induced hazards							■					
Science and technological in local, national, and global challenges							■	■	■	■		
History and Nature of Science												
Science as a human endeavor						■	■	■	■	■		
Nature of scientific knowledge						■	■	■	■	■		
Historical perspectives						■	■	■	■	■		

Mathematics, Statistics, and the Graphing Calculator

PURPOSE

Mathematics is known as the only true and universal language. It is the foundation of science. This chapter is an introduction to the statistics and mathematics needed in this book as well as instructions for features of the graphing calculator. The graphing calculator used in the book is the TI-83 Plus (and on occasion the Silver edition) but any graphing calculator with regression features can be used. The data collection device used is the CBL-2. Some probes come with the CBL-2, but others that may be needed can be obtained through Vernier or Flinn Scientific.

If you have completed algebra, most of the material in this book is within your range of mathematical knowledge. The mathematical concepts will be explained as needed in the chapters that follow. Mathematical modeling and dimensional analysis to solve problems are used extensively in this book. The mathematics core examines the topics of decimal and scientific notation, metric conversions, ratios and proportions, rates of change, various forms of graphing, geometric shapes, basic trigonometry, and several mathematical functions. The functions explored are linear, exponential, quadratic, cubic, logarithmic, inverse, and trigonometric. If you have not studied all of these, brief explanations are included in the appropriate chapters.

Descriptive statistics is extensively used in this book as well as different types of regression. No inferential statistics processes are used. We will now discuss the statistical concepts students need in this book.

FOUNDATIONS

Definitions

Population is the entire collection of individuals or objects to be studied.

Sample is a subset of the population.

Variable is a characteristic of the individuals or objects whose value may change.

Datum (data, plural form) is the result from making an observation on one (univariate), two (bivariate), or more variables.

Examples of **qualitative data** include categorical information such as color, gender, and so forth.

Examples of **quantitative data** include numerical measurements from entities such as temperature and height.

Data should come from random samples and you need to make at least three measurements to obtain the mean.

One-Variable Data

One-variable data is just as it sounds. You collect data that are only associated with a single variable. For example, heights of students in your class or the number of desks in a classroom describe a single thing that you want to talk about. There are calculations that can be made and graphs that can be created once the one-variable data have been collected.

Measures of Central Tendency for One-Variable Data

1. Sample mean:

$$\bar{x} = \frac{\text{Sum of all observations in the sample}}{\text{Number of observations in the sample}} = \frac{\sum x}{n}$$

2. Sample median is obtained by first ordering the n observations from smallest to largest and including every value, even if the value is repeated. The sample median is the single middle value if n is odd or the mean of the middle two values if n is even.
3. Mode is the value that appears the most often.

Measures of Deviation for One-Variable Data

1. Range = maximum value − minimum value.
2. Sample variance:

$$s^2 = \frac{\sum (x - \bar{x})^2}{n - 1}$$

3. Sample standard deviation:

$$s = \sqrt{s^2}$$

4. Quartile 1 = Q1 = median of the lower half of the sample.
5. Quartile 3 = Q3 = median of the upper half of the sample.
6. Interquartile range = IQR = Q3 − Q1.
7. Outlier is an observation that is more than 1.5(IQR) above Q3 or 1.5(IQR) below Q1.

Boxplot.   A boxplot is a graph that displays the following five values: minimum, Q1, median, Q3, and maximum.

To construct a boxplot:

1. Draw a horizontal measurement scale.
2. Construct a rectangular box whose left side is Q1 and right side is Q3.
3. Draw a vertical line segment inside the box at the median.
4. Extend a vertical line from each end of the box to the minimum and maximum values.

Most graphing calculators have a boxplot feature that will plot the graph for you with these five values. However, it is important that you also know how to construct one by hand.

Example. The following are final exam grades for a mathematics class:

86 75 90 80 66 57 99 87 84 77 68 29 93 87 74 72 79 81

Use the graphing calculator, or calculate by hand, the answers to the following:

Mean =   Median =   Mode =   Standard deviation =

Range =   Q1 =   Q3 =   IQR =

Check your results with the answers below.

Mean	Median	Mode	Standard deviation
= 76.9	= 79.5	= 87	= 15.7
Range = 70	Q1 = 72	Q3 = 87	IQR = 15

Draw the boxplot. Your boxplot should look like the one shown in Figure 1.1. Are there any outliers? Why or why not?

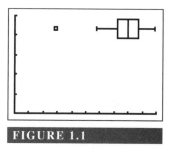

FIGURE 1.1

You can see from the boxplot on the calculator that there is an outlier and that it occurs at data point 29. The outlier can be calculated by hand by taking 1.5 times the IQR of 15, giving you 22.5. Next, take 22.5 and subtract it from the value for Q1, or 72. When you take 72 − 22.5, you get 49.5. This result tells you that any data points smaller than 49.5 will be outliers. The data point less than 49.5 in this example is 29. To verify that there are no outliers at the upper end of our boxplot, we can compute Q3 + 22.5, resulting in 109.5. Because there are no data points larger than 109.5, there are no outliers at the upper end of this data set.

Two-Variable Data

One-variable data was concerned with a single piece of information. In contrast, two-variable data link two pieces of information together. If you collect data regarding the water level in a graduated cylinder at a particular time, then you are dealing with two-variable data. Time is one variable, and water level is the other. Notice that the water level is dependent on time. Not only are the two variables linked, but also one is dependent on the other. You can calculate statistics such as mean or standard deviation for each individual data set, but many times you will not be interested in doing so. Most often, you will want to graph the data and calculate a line or curve that will best fit the data.

Scatterplot.　A scatterplot is a graph of bivariate data that has an x and a y variable. Each observation is represented by a point on a rectangular coordinate system. The x-axis represents the explanatory, or independent variable and the y-axis represents the response or the dependent variable. Scatterplots can represent various types of relationships such as linear, quadratic, exponential, or no relationship. As with the boxplot, scatterplots can be done on the calculator. Throughout this book, you will be asked to construct scatterplots by hand on graph paper and then verify your results using the calculator.

Linear Regression.　We will use the calculator's regression features instead of calculating the linear regression equations by hand. Pearson's correlation coefficient (r) is a common measure of the strength of a linear relationship. The correlation coefficient r can range from -1 to $+1$, inclusive. The graphing calculator displays r when the linear regression equation is calculated.

General linear equation: $y = ax + b$ where a = slope and b = y-intercept.

Example.　Suppose you measure your child's height (in cm) at various ages (in months) and obtain the following information. It would make sense that as your child ages, his height would increase. We call age the *explanatory variable* because it explains or helps predict the height. Height is called the *response variable* because that is the information that is collected at a certain age. In other words, once you decide at what age you will collect the information, the only thing left to do is record the height. Height is also referred to as the *dependent variable* because it is dependent on your explanatory variable, also known as the *independent variable* (the thing you have control over).

The following two-variable data set was collected and recorded below.

Age (months)	Height (cm)
36	84
48	89
51	91
53	92
57	94
60	96

In order to enter data sets into the calculator, you must do the following. Before you begin, you may want to clear some of the lists already entered. To clear existing data, press [STAT] and EDIT will be highlighted, press [4], press [2nd] [1] (to get L1), press [,] [2nd][2] for L2 and continue for any of the six lists you want cleared with commas between each L. When you have selected the lists you want cleared, press [ENTER] and the calculator will say DONE. Now you may begin entering new data. Press [STAT], [1] then enter the data. To move between lists, use the right or left arrows. To correct entries, use the up and down arrows. When the previous data set is entered into L1 and L2, it looks like Figure 1.2.

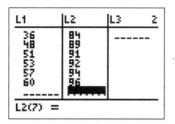

FIGURE 1.2

To get a scatterplot on your calculator, you should set up the STATPLOT screen as shown in Figure 1.3. If we use these data to graph the scatterplot, we get the graph represented in Figure 1.4 by using an appropriate window.

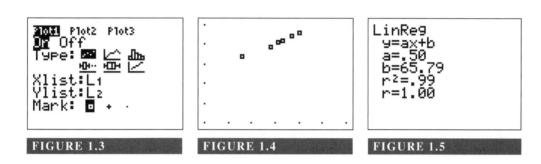

FIGURE 1.3   FIGURE 1.4   FIGURE 1.5

Because the data appear to be linear, we want to calculate the linear regression for this data set to see how well the data are correlated and to get a prediction equation. The equation $y = .5x + 65.79$ (Figure 1.5) can be used to make several interpretations of the data. First, we can use it as a predictor for future height. For example, if we want to predict the height of the child at 65 months, we can substitute 65 for x and find the corresponding y value. The predicted height will be 98.29 cm. This process can be used for any value for age, but we must be careful not to stray too far from our original data. When we get too far away from the original data points, there is a greater chance for inaccuracy because we are extrapolating from the original information.

You can get the value of 98.29 from your calculator by following these steps. When you use the LinReg command, add Y1 to the end of the command so that your screen looks like Figure 1.6. This will put the linear regression equation into Y1, and you can then graph the regression line along with the scatterplot (Figure 1.7). By tracing on the line, you can determine height values for any of the age values in your window (Figure 1.8).

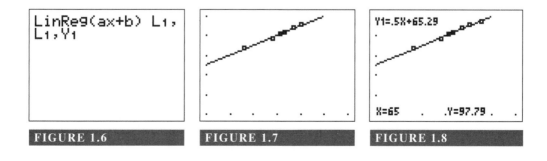

FIGURE 1.6   FIGURE 1.7   FIGURE 1.8

The other useful thing about the regression equation of $y = .5x + 65.79$ is that it allows us to interpret the meaning of the data and the equation. The slope of 0.5 means that for every increase of one month age, the height will increase by 0.5 cm. Remember that slope is the change in y over the change in x. In our problem, x is age and y is height. The y-intercept of 65.79 also allows us to make an interpretation about the data. This means that if age is 0, then height will be 65.29 cm. There are 2.54 cm in 1 in., which means that a newborn would be approximately 25.7 inches long. This is a little unreasonable, but at least we know how to interpret the y-intercept for this problem and we can now make that same interpretation for other problems in the book.

INVESTIGATION

Materials

> one paper or styrofoam cup
> paper clip
> graduated cylinder, 100 mL
> timer with second hand
> graphing calculator

Procedure

1. Fill the cylinder with water until volume can be read. Always read the volume at the bottom of the meniscus.
2. Make a hole on the bottom of the cup using the paper clip, put your finger over the hole, and fill the cup with water.
3. Release the water and record the volume of the water every 5 seconds for 1 minute. Be sure the water is dripping steadily but not too quickly. If the water is dripping too quickly, ask your instructor for an additional cup and try again.
4. Record the volumes on the table and then complete the worksheet.

Data Table

Time									
Volume									
Time									
Volume									

REFLECTIONS AND EXTENSIONS

1. Use the graphing calculator to graph the scatterplot, then sketch the scatterplot below.

2. What type of relationship do the data appear to have?

3. Use the calculator to fit the regression equation. What is the equation and what is r? Interpret the regression equation in words related to the problem.

4. Use the calculator to find the following for the volume data:

   Mean =   Standard deviation =   Median =

   Q1 =   Q3 =   Range =   IQR =

5. Sketch the boxplot below.

6. Are there any outliers? Why or why not?

7. Develop your own two-variable data set of at least 10 values. The variables selected can be anything you choose, and the data can be invented. Define both variables and identify which variable is the dependent and independent data source. Next enter the values into your calculator and complete the following tasks: sketch the scatterplot; identify the type of relationship; give the regression equation and identify the mean, median, and mode.

CHAPTER TWO

Problem Solving and Dimensional Analysis

PURPOSE

This investigation starts with the basic concepts of dimensional analysis and significant digits and then demonstrates their use in scientific problem solving. We will discuss the use of scientific notation for the reporting of data and rules that govern calculations for the mathematical operations of addition/subtraction and multiplication/division along with the distinction between accuracy and precision. Rules of exponents are explained, and the use of these rules with scientific notation is demonstrated. Throughout this book, you will use the fundamental concepts presented in this chapter.

FOUNDATIONS

Dimensional Analysis

Dimensional analysis is a mathematical manipulation technique that allows problem solvers to organize given information without the memorization of specific algorithms. Dimensional analysis is sometimes referred to as the factor-label or unit analysis method because it makes use of unit factors (e.g., 1 in. = 2.54 cm). This technique is a simple method used to convert measurements from a given unit to a requested unit, and it makes the decision for the question "Do I multiply or divide by the conversion factor?" instinctive. You simply set up a unit fraction to make sure the units (labels) in the numerator divide out with corresponding units (labels) in the denominator. The use of labels (e.g., meters, seconds, miles per hour) is just as important as the factors used for the conversions.

Below is an example of how to use dimensional analysis (factor-label method) to convert 12 miles to kilometers.

$$\frac{12 \text{ mi}}{} \left| \frac{5280 \text{ ft}}{1 \text{ mi}} \right| \frac{12 \text{ in}}{1 \text{ ft}} \left| \frac{2.54 \text{ cm}}{1 \text{ in}} \right| \frac{1 \text{ m}}{100 \text{ cm}} \left| \frac{1 \text{ km}}{1000 \text{ m}} \right.$$

$$= 19.312 \text{ km} = 19 \text{ km}$$

Significant Digits

In this book, we will report answers first in decimal notation, then using significant digits. In the previous problem, all the conversion factors are considered to contain an infinite number of decimal places (i.e., they are precise measurements). In science, rules for determining significant digits govern how data are reported. You can never report a solution to a problem that involves only multiplication and division to a greater number of digits than the least number of significant digits in the problem. For addition and subtraction, the rule is a little different. In the above case, assume you can never report a value that is less certain than your least certain measurement (i.e., when comparing 1.001 to 1.0010, there are, respectively, 4 and 5 significant digits, giving the latter value greater certainty). The value 1.0010 has greater certainty as compared to 1.001 because it contains a significant digit in the ten-thousandths place, one place beyond 1.001. Another way to look at reporting the data to the correct number of significant digits when adding or subtracting is to limit the number of decimal places by finding the leftmost significant digit among all the values in your problem.

Rules for Usage of Significant Digits
1. All nonzero numbers are significant.
2. Zeros between significant digits are significant.
3. Final zeros that follow a decimal point are significant.
4. All other zeros are placeholders (i.e., not significant).

When determining significant digits for a measurement, never start counting significant digits until you reach the first nonzero number. For example, 0.00000000001 has many decimal places but only one significant digit (the last digit). If the number in question does not have a decimal point, then begin in the units place and go left until you read the first nonzero number. All the digits from here to the left are considered significant. The count of nonzero numbers will tell you how many significant digits are present. For example, 270,000 carries two significant digits (sd). Below you will find five examples of mathematical operations in compliance with the rules for reporting factors and labels discussed above.

Some calculators are also able to determine the number of significant figures in a measurement. To get to the SIG-FIG CALCULATOR on the TI-83 Plus Silver Edition, press the APPS key, and arrow down to SciTools, which will bring up another menu called SELECT A TOOL. Press 1 to obtain the SIG-FIG CALCULATOR. Determine the significant digits in the following values:

1. 876 g
2. 640 mL
3. 0.0089 m
4. 8003 s
5. 760. mmHg

[Answers: 3, 2, 2, 4, 3]

Multiplication and Division Examples

$$4.53 \text{ cm} \times 0.089 \text{ cm} \times 2.09 \text{ cm} = 0.8426 \text{ cm}^3 = 0.84 \text{ cm}^3$$

The first term has 3 sd, the second term has 2 sd and the third terms has 3 sd. Therefore, the answer will have 2 sd (the least number of significant digits).

$$\frac{5.23 \times 10^4 \text{ m}}{(0.5 \text{ s})(1.0 \text{ s})} = \frac{1.046 \times 10^5 \text{ m}}{\text{s}^2} = 1 \times 10^5 \text{ m/s}^2$$

(A discussion of how to enter scientific notation in your calculator is found in the next section.) The lowest number of significant digits in this problem is 1 (0.5). So your answer should have 1 sd.

Addition and Subtraction Examples

10.349 g	39.32 g
+7.76 g	−31.113 g
18.109 g = 18.11 g	8.207 g = 8.21 g

Note that the value with the leftmost significant digit in the addition problem is the 6 in 7.76 and the value with the leftmost significant digit in the subtraction problem is the 2 in 39.32. For practice, repeat the previous exercises to confirm these values using your graphing calculator.

Combination of Operations Example

$$\frac{10.6 \text{ g/L} - 10. \text{ g/L}}{10. \text{ g/L}} \times 100 = \frac{1 \text{ g/L}}{10. \text{ g/L}} \times 100 = 10\%$$

Note the decimal following the number 10 in the problem above (10.). When a measurement is written as such, this is a special notation used to imply that the final zero of the measurement is a significant digit.

Greater certainty of a measurement is possible when a more accurate instrument is available. Improved instrumentation allows you to increase your accuracy and precision. **Accuracy** answers the question of how close to the standard for that measurement did you come. **Precision** is concerned with the number of times you acquired the same measurement. Of course, every measurement has error associated with it (no measured quantity is ever exact!), and don't forget, all measurements must have labels—*no naked numbers*!

Scientific Notation

You can see from some of the previous examples that numbers can be written in different ways. One way is scientific notation. Recall that **scientific notation** is a number greater than or equal to 1 and less than 10 multiplied by 10 to some power. Any number, when written in scientific notation has the number of significant digits present in the number before the 10. Another case in which significant digits can be determined by the way the number is written, is when there is a lack of certainty in the number. For example, if you are asked to determine the number of significant digits in 100, you might question whether the final zeros are significant or just placeholders. To counteract this doubt, if you see the number written as 100. (with the decimal point present), then the value is said to contain three significant digits. Likewise, if you are asked to express the value of 100 with two significant digits you can write it in scientific notation, 1.0×10^2, or you can use a special notation by placing a line above the first 0 in 100 or 10̄0. Counts (e.g., 15 beakers or 7 desks) and conversion factors (e.g., 1 m = 100 cm) are said to have an infinite number of significant digits and consequently do not influence the number of significant digits reported as the solution to a problem.

To do scientific notation problems on your calculator, you must make use of your exponential key. The exponential key looks different on different calculators. The examples below show how you can use your calculator to enter scientific notation.

Example.   Multiply 5×10^4 by 6×10^9.

You would first press 5, press the [EE] button, press 4, press [X], press 6, press [EE], press 9, then press [ENTER] to obtain 3E14 as the answer. You should report the answer as 3×10^{14}. (*Note:* This problem is also very easy to do using the rules of exponents explained in the next section.)

Example.   Multiply by 5×10^4 by 6×10^9 (same problem as above, but using different keystrokes).

You would first press 5, press [10^x] button, press 4, press [X], press 6, press [10^x] button, press 9, then press [ENTER] to obtain 3E14 as the answer. It needs to be noted that either of these methods can lead to confusion for students who assume that they need to press the "multiply" button on their calculators more than once to complete the problem. When you press [EE] or [10^x] the calculator accepts the entry as one value and there is no need to hit the "multiply" button unless you are doing a multiplication problem. If you do, then you will get an answer that is a factor of 10 greater than you anticipate for each entry. Only hit the multiply button when you want to perform the operation of multiplication.

Exponents

The rules of exponents are used in conjunction with scientific notation and are important to know. When working with very large or very small numerical values, calculators express the answers in scientific notation. Below is an example to illustrate how scientific notation is displayed on a calculator.

Example.   Multiply 100,000,150 times 548,000,628.

Note that the display shows 5.4800145E16, as in Figure 2.1. This is the calculator's method for writing 5.4800145×10^{16}. Also note that the calculator loses some certainty in the problem. It is best to enter a problem in scientific notation, so as not to lose any certainty in the final answer. The first number entered, 100,000,150, has eight significant digits and 548,000,628 contains nine. Therefore, the answer should have eight digits in it. In this case the display is correct, but most calculators are not programmed to adhere to rules of significant digits—it is up to you to record your answers with the correct number of significant digits!

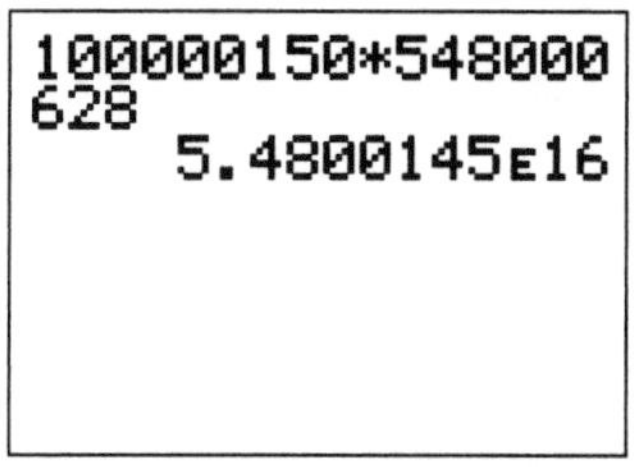

```
100000150*548000
628
        5.4800145E16
```

FIGURE 2.1

Below are examples of multiplication problems using scientific notation.

Example. Multiply 106,800,000 times 38,700,000,000.

You should record your answer using three significant digits and in scientific notation: 4.13×10^{18} (Figure 2.2).

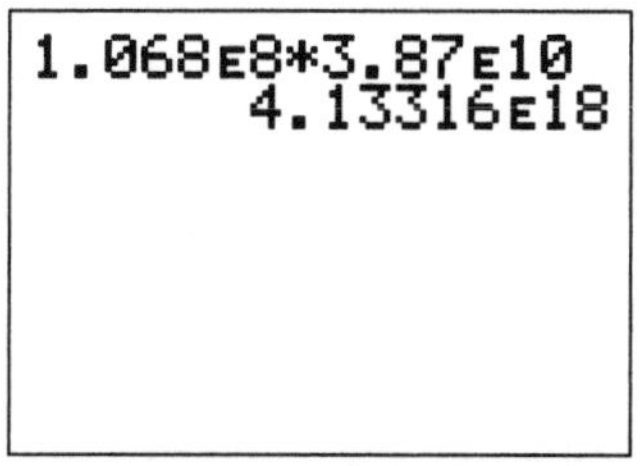

```
1.068E8*3.87E10
        4.13316E18
```

FIGURE 2.2

Example. Multiply 0.000 547 1 times 0.000 000 000 000 002 018.

Because both factors contain four significant digits, the correctly written answer is 1.104×10^{-18} (Figure 2.3).

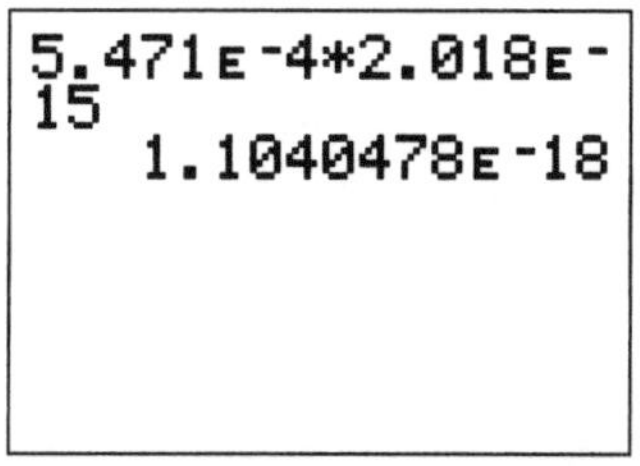

```
5.471E-4*2.018E-
15
        1.1040478E-18
```

FIGURE 2.3

Students can perform many conversions without using a calculator or paper and pencil if they understand scientific notation and the rules of exponents.

Rules.   If m and n are integers and a, b, and c are real numbers, then:

Product rule for exponents:	$a^m a^n = a^{m+n}$
Power rule for exponents:	$(a^m)^n = a^{mn}$
Quotient rule of exponents:	$\dfrac{a^m}{a^n} = a^{m-n}, \qquad a \neq 0$
Zero exponent:	$a^0 = 1, \qquad a \neq 0$
Negative exponent:	$a^{-n} = \dfrac{1}{a^n}, \qquad a \neq 0$

The following examples can be used to illustrate the use of the rules of exponents.

Example.   Multiply 4.0×10^{-5} by $1.2 \times 10^{12} = 4.8 \times 10^7$.
You multiply 4.0 by 1.2 to obtain 4.8. Then use the rules of exponents and add –5 to 12 to get 7.

Example.   Divide 6×10^{10} by $3 \times 10^4 = 2 \times 10^6$.
When you divide 6 by 3, you get 2. The rules of exponents indicate the need to subtract the exponents. Therefore, $10 - 4$ gives 6.

INVESTIGATION

The purpose of this investigation is to practice the dimensional analysis technique used for problem solving in this book. It will be somewhat different from the formats in other chapters because the goals here are to build skills and to become familiar with techniques that are used throughout the book.
From any equality that states a relationship between two units of measure, you can find two conversion factors. For example, 1 ft = 12 in. Because these quantities are equivalent measurements, a ratio between them is equivalent to 1.

$$\frac{12 \text{ in}}{1 \text{ ft}} \quad \text{and} \quad \frac{1 \text{ ft}}{12 \text{ in}}$$

(Remember: anything divided by itself is 1. Hence, these are sometimes called *unit factors* because the ratio is equivalent to 1.) These relationships are also known as *conversion factors*. Conversion factors include the following:

1000 g = 1 kg	453.6 g = 1 lb	1 k = .200 g
1000 mm = 1 m	100 cm = 1 m	1 m = 10^9 nm
1 link = 7.92 in.	1 chain = 100 links	1 furlong = 10 chains
2.54 cm = 1 in.	1 ft = 12 in.	5280 ft = 1 mi
1 yd = 3 ft	1 hr = 60 min	1 min = 60 s
1000 mL = 1 L	1 cm^3 = 1 mL	1 J = 1 kg m^2 s^{-2}

Some calculators have conversion factors built in or accessible from an application downloaded from the Internet. If your calculator has these capabilities, you can confirm the answers you get doing the problems by hand by using your calculator to check your answers.

If you have the TI-83 Plus Silver edition calculator, then return to the instructions on how to access SciTools. This time press 2:UNIT CON-VERTER and ENTER. Several choices for conversions will appear. While working the problems below, confirm your answers using this function.

Example.   Convert 76.8 g to kg.

Select MASS. Arrow over to "g" and enter 76.8. Now arrow back to "kg" and press ENTER. The answer displayed should read: 0.0768 kg.

PRACTICE PROBLEMS

Perform the following conversions. Give your answers in both decimal and scientific notation.

1. How many kilograms are there in 125 g of a substance?

2. Find the number of centimeters in 5 km.

3. How many meters are there in 5.0 km?

4. Find the number of milligrams in 0.5 kg.

5. Convert 500. m to kilometers.

6. How many cubic centimeters are there in 2.20 L?

7. Find the number of millimeters in 6.98 cm.

8. How many liters are equal to 2700 mL?

9. Suppose you ran the 100-yd dash in 10. s. Determine your speed in miles per hour.

10. A solid metal sphere has a volume of 3.2 ft^3. The mass of the sphere is 255 lb. Find the density of the metal sphere in grams per cubic centimeter. [$d = m/V$] Will the metal sphere sink or float in water? Why?

ADDITIONAL PROBLEMS

Solve the following problems. Always use significant digits. Failure to show work will result in minimal credit!

1. How many significant digits are in the following?
   a. 20 ft
   b. 20. ft
   c. 20.0 ft
   d. 20 victories
   e. 20

2. How many wheels are there in 4 dozen tricycles?

3. If 2000 students are enrolled and each room holds exactly 20 students, how many rooms are needed?

4. The Sears Tower in Chicago is 1454 ft tall. How high is this in meters?

5. How many feet will a snail travel in 5.6 hr if it moves at an average speed of 1.1 in./min?

6. The Kentucky Derby is a horse race of 10-furlongs. (*Hint:* assume a perfect furlong.) How many miles is this?

7. A professional pitcher can easily throw the ball over the plate at 95.8 mph. Convert this measurement into SI standard units, m/s.

8. Find the volume of the Hope Diamond, given that the density of diamond (carbon) is 3.51 g/cm^3 and the weight is 44 karats.

9. If a pure gold crown weighs 2280 g and has a volume of 115 cm^3, find the density of the metal in the crown in g/cm^3.

10. A student finds a gold-colored, heavy rock having a mass of 22.0 g. The student fills a graduated cylinder with water to exactly 10.0 cm^3. When the rock is placed in the water, the new volume in the cylinder is 13.8 cm^3. The density of pure gold is 19.3 g/cm^3. Is the rock pure gold? (Justify your answer mathematically. You might need to refer to another chapter!)

11. An ice skating rink is 150. ft × 60. ft, covered with a 1.0 in. layer of ice. What is the total weight of ice in pounds, if the density of the ice is 0.92 g/cm^3. Why does ice float?

12. In 1924 the French physicist Louis de Broglie made the somewhat startling suggestion that all moving particles, from electrons to city buses, have a wavelength, λ. That wavelength is determined by the formula with constant h = 6.63 × 10^{-34} J·s, the particle mass, m, and the velocity, v:

$$\lambda = \frac{h}{mv}$$

What is the wavelength (in nanometers) of a 150. g baseball thrown by a pitcher at 90. mph?

CHAPTER THREE

Fundamental and Derived Units of Measurement

PURPOSE

This investigation will cover the distinction between fundamental and derived units of measurements, percentage error, precision error, and intensive and extensive physical properties of matter (e.g., density, specific heat capacity, length, mass, and volume).

FOUNDATIONS

Fundamental and Derived Measurements

Some of the **fundamental** (directly measured) standards of measurements are seen in Table 3.1. Scientists have agreed on certain "housed" standards to communicate experimental results obtained under different conditions in comparable ways. Examples of most of these measurements are kept in special places like the International Bureau of Weights and Measures in Sèvres, France. The mole is also considered to be a fundamental quantity. A **mole** is a count of the number of particles found in a particular amount of a substance. Specifically, the mole is equal to 6.0221×10^{23} "particles." Examples of particles are ions, atoms, molecules, grains of sand, footballs, or little furry creatures called moles! If you can count it, you can eventually have a

TABLE 3.1 Measurements and Standards

MEASUREMENT	INSTRUMENT	STANDARD	SYMBOL
length	meter stick	meter	m
mass	balance	kilogram	kg
time	clock, watch	second	s
temperature	thermometer	kelvin	K
mole	none	mole	mol

mole of it. However, this is a little naïve. The actual counting of a value this large (602,210,000,000,000,000,000,000) is virtually impossible. The size of a mole is determined by indirect measurements.

When using a calibrated instrument (such as a ruler or graduated cylinder), it is generally accepted that you estimate only one decimal place beyond what you have indicator marks for. In other words, if you are dealing with a ruler marked in centimeters, you can estimate a measurement that falls in between two centimeter marks. In this case, you can report a measurement that falls halfway between 2 and 3 cm as 2.5 cm, but you cannot report a measurement of 2.50 cm. To report this measurement you would have to have markings on the ruler indicative of millimeters. Likewise, if you have a graduated cylinder marked by units, then you can determine the volume of your liquid to the tenths place. (Don't forget to measure the volume of liquids in a graduated cylinder from the bottom of the meniscus, and always report a measurement with the greatest certainty allowed.)

Derived units use relationships between fundamental measurements (e.g., the label for speed is written in terms of meters/second = m/s). Remember that no measured quantity is ever exact! If you measure a quantity to four significant digits, three are certain and the last is always an estimate. If you have a more accurate instrument, then you can obtain a more certain measurement. Other examples of derived measurements include specific heat capacity, which is calculated in terms of energy divided by the product of the mass of an object and its heat intensity (cal/g °C, J/g °C), and density, which is determined from a ratio of mass to volume (g/cm^3, g/mL). For certain derived measurements, known values are assumed to be accurate. For example, the density of distilled water at 3.98 °C is agreed by convention to be 1.00 g/cm^3.

Percentage Error

When you determine by experimentation the density of distilled water to be more or less than 1.00 g/cm^3, then you should calculate a percentage error for your calculation. The following formula is used to determine the amount of error associated with the mean of your measurement.

$$\left| \frac{\text{Expected value} - \text{Experimental value}}{\text{Expected value}} \right| \times 100 = \text{Percentage error}$$

All measured quantities have errors associated with them. Your accuracy is determined by how close your measured or counted value gets to the accepted standard value. Precision is related to the instrument used to obtain the measurement. If you are being precise, you are able to repeat the measurement numerable times. You can be precise (get the same measurement repeatedly) and not be accurate (get a value close to the accepted or true value) when you use an instrument that is not calibrated properly or is not working properly. Also, the accuracy of your measurement depends on the capacity and sensitivity of your instrument.

Mass (reported in kg, g, mg, etc.) is an example of a fundamental measurement; however, weight is reported in terms of force, a derived unit, newton (N) or kg·m/s^2. You obtain the mass of an object by using a balance to compare the object's unknown mass to a known mass. You determine weight by using a scale to measure the force between two bodies. The force of gravity changes when the distance between the center of the object being weighed and the center of the Earth changes. Hence weight is dependent on the location of the object being weighed. The weight of a 60-N object at sea level is less when measured on a very tall mountain, but a mass of 60 kg is the same in both locations. An object weighs less on the moon than on the Earth because the moon has a smaller radius, but the object's mass is the same regardless of location.

Precision Error

Another important type of reported error is related to the precision of measured values. This is sometimes referred to as precision error and is dependent on your instrument. The easiest way to describe this type of error is by way of example. Let's say that you weighed a small stone four times. The values obtained are reported below:

$$m_1 = 1.56 \text{ g}$$
$$m_2 = 1.58 \text{ g}$$
$$m_3 = 1.55 \text{ g}$$
$$m_4 = 1.61 \text{ g}$$
$$\frac{1.56 \text{ g} + 1.58 \text{ g} + 1.55 \text{ g} + 1.61 \text{ g}}{4} = 1.575 \text{ g} = 1.58 \text{ g}$$

The mean (average) mass is the sum of these four measurements divided by 4. Recall from Chapter 2 the rules for reporting significant digits when adding and subtracting are a little different from the rules used for multiplying and dividing. In the previous case, regardless of the number of significant digits in any one measurement, you report your answer to the hundredth's place because your least accurate measurement is reported to the hundredth's place. In this case, all the values are reported to the hundredth's place. (*Note:* the 4 in the denominator is a count of the number of values used and has an infinite number of significant digits, so it does not affect the reporting of the mean number of significant digits. The fraction bar acts as a separator for the rules that govern the adding in the numerator and the division needed to complete the calculation.) After determining the mean, you need to calculate the average error in order to report the precision error.

Masses	**| Individual Error from Mean |** $\lvert m_i - \text{mean} \rvert$
$m_1 = 1.56$	0.02
$m_2 = 1.58$	0.00
$m_3 = 1.55$	0.03
$m_4 = 1.61$	0.03
	$\Sigma = 0.08$

$$\text{Average error} = \frac{0.08}{4} = \pm 0.02$$

This type of uncertainty calculation determines the sensitivity of your instrument. When this error is large in comparison to the size of the measurement, you need to find a more sensitive measurement or recalibrate your instrument. In this case, our average mass reported with the precision error is 1.58 ± .02 g.

Intensive and Extensive Physical Properties

Specific heat capacity and density are **intensive** physical properties that can be used to help identify an unknown element (they do not vary with the amount of substance you have). All chemical elements have densities and specific heat capacities that are unique to them. In other words, if you can determine the density of an element, this property will aid you in its identification. **Extensive** physical properties are those that concern the amount of substance you have (mass, volume) and also properties such as its velocity or cost. You do not have control over the intensive physical properties such as color, hardness, melting point, boiling point, density, refractive index, specific heat capacity, but you are usually able to control the extensive properties of a substance.

INVESTIGATION

Materials

    3 × 5 index card

    scissors

    meter stick

    graphing calculator

    graduated cylinder, 10 mL

    shallow tray (pizza tray)

    pipet (eyedropper)

    foil

    unknown liquids A, B, and C

    lycopodium powder*

    stearic acid solution**

    small stone

    protractor

Part One: Open Ended

1. You may collaborate with a partner to obtain this measurement.
2. Determine the height (in meters) of the building in which you are meeting.
3. Repeat the measurement two additional times, using the same procedure.
4. While outside pick up a small stone for Part Five!

---

*Some people may be allergic to these spores. An alternative is the use of sulfur powder or chalk dust.

**Stearic acid is dissolved in cyclohexane; the concentration = 0.15 g/L. Oleic acid dissolved in ethanol may be used as a substitute.

Part Two: Directed and Discovery

1. Obtain a rectangular piece of foil. (*Note:* any foil may be used for this procedure; aluminum is usually the most assessable.) Measure the mass (in grams to as many places as your instrument allows), length (in centimeters), and width (in centimeters) of the foil. Use the known density to calculate the thickness of your foil.

2. Next fold the foil as tightly as possible. Determine the volume of your foil by water displacement. Calculate the density.

Part Three: Directed

Note: You must perform this investigation on a night of a full moon!

1. Cut a 2.5 cm square notch in one edge or in the middle of a 3 × 5 index card.
2. Tape the card to a window where you can see the moon.
3. Align the meter stick at a 90° angle with the card.
4. Look at the moon through the notch.
5. While sliding the meter stick through your fingers, back away from the window until the moon fills the area of the notch.
6. Hold the end of the meter stick up to your eyes so that you can measure the distance (in centimeters) between the notch and your eye.
7. Multiply the distance by 3475 km, then divide by 2.5 cm. The results will approximate the distance from the Earth to the moon in kilometers, or about 384,400 km.
8. Repeat this process an additional two times.

Part Four: Verification

1. Fill a shallow tray with distilled water.
2. Lightly coat the surface of the water with lycopodium powder.
3. Add a drop of the stearic acid solution (a solution of oleic acid can be substituted) from a height of approximately 25 cm to the surface of the powdered water. (The solvent evaporates, and the stearic acid spreads out on the water surface. The film's boundary is easy to see because it pushes back the lycopodium powder).
4. Measure the "circle" resulting from the drop of solution in three directions and take an average of your measurements to determine the average diameter.
5. Add a second drop and make three measurements of the new diameter, then add a third drop and find the average diameter.
6. A "monolayer" is formed because the long carbon chains of the stearic acid are hydrophobic (they extend out of the water) and only the organic acid functional group (–COOH) is inserted into the water.
7. Determine the number of drops of solution required to fill a 10-cm^3 (10 mL) graduated cylinder to the 1-mL mark. Verify the value by counting the number of drops required to continue filling the cylinder to the 2-mL mark.

Part Five: Directed and Predictive

1. Determine the density of the small stone you obtained in Part One. Report this value in g/cm^3.
2. Determine the densities of liquids A, B, and C. Use a volume of 50 mL of each liquid.
3. Pour all three liquids into one 250-mL beaker.
4. Predict where the stone will settle when it is dropped into the liquids.
5. Drop the stone into the beaker of liquids. Was your prediction correct?

REFLECTIONS AND EXTENSIONS

Part One

1. Obtain an average of your group's collected measurements.
2. Record your group's average measurement on the blackboard for other groups to use.
3. Determine the mean, median, and mode of the data obtained by the other groups.
4. Report your data in the Data Table that follows.

Data Table for Part One

Average height of building: _____ (from your group)

Record your height on the blackboard for other groups to use in calculating the collaborative statistics. Make sure to include a label with your measurement and as many digits as your instrument allows (you can estimate only one digit beyond the calibrations available.)

Briefly describe your procedure.

Class Data

Mean: _____   Median: _____   Mode: _____

Part Two

1. Determine the precision error for your mass measurements.
2. Calculate the thickness of your piece of foil using the directions in Part One. Report your answer in centimeters and inches. (Known densities: Al = 2.70 g/cm^3, Cu = 8.92 g/cm^3, Sn = 7.28 g/cm^3, and Zn = 7.13 g/cm^3.)
3. Calculate the density of your foil using water displacement (Archimedes' Principle) to determine the volume. How does it compare to the expected value? Calculate the percentage error of your experimental density.
4. Report your results in the Data Table that follows.

Data Table for Part Two

Mass

m_1 = _____ m_2 = _____ m_3 = _____

average mass = _____

Calculate the precision error of your masses.

Precision Error = _____ ± _____

Length = _____ in.   Width = _____ in.

Thickness = _____ in.

Show calculations for determination of foil thickness and for the conversion.

Volume = _____ mL   Thickness = _____ cm

Show your calculation for the percentage error of your experimental density.

Experimental density = _____

Percentage error = _____

Part Three

1. Convert the mean distance you obtained to miles. (Compare to the known value.) Report your answer using the correct number of significant digits and in scientific notation.
2. Convert the mean distance in miles to light-years for the moon investigation. (Light travels at a speed of 3.00×10^8 m/s = 186,000 mi/s.) Report your answer using the correct number of significant digits and in scientific notation.
3. Report your data and calculations in the Data Table that follows.

Data Table for Part Three

Average distance between the notch and your eye: _____

Average distance between the Earth and moon: _____ km

Convert the distance in kilometers to miles.

Calculate the percentage error. (Known mean distance, Earth to moon = 3.84×10^8 m)

Convert the distance in miles to light-years.

Part Four

1. Report the average diameter of the circles formed by the lycopodium powder.
2. Determine the average area covered by the stearic acid drop. Area = $\pi d^2/4$.
3. Record the number of drops per mL (cm^3) of solution.
4. Find the mass of stearic acid in one drop of solution. (The concentration of stearic acid is 0.15 g/L and its density is 0.85 g/cm^3.)
5. Complete the Data Table and calculations.

Data Table for Part Four

	1 drop	**2 drops**	**3 drops**
Diameter 1			
Diameter 2			
Diameter 3			
Avg Diameter			

Area covered by 1 drop = _____ cm^2

Area covered by 2 drops = _____ cm^2

Area covered by 3 drops = _____ cm^2

Area/1 drop = _____ cm^2

Area/2 drops = _____ cm^2

Area/3 drops = _____ cm^2

(*Note:* these areas should be approximately the same size. This confirms that stearic acid is forming a monolayer on the top of the water.)

Average area/drop = _____ cm^2

How many drops did it take to fill a volume of 1 mL? _____ drops/mL

Determine the volume of solution per drop (this is the reciprocal of the above count).

Volume/drop of solution = _____ cm^3

The concentration of stearic acid is 0.15 g/L. Remember that 1 L = 1000 cm^3. Using the volume you recorded and the density of the acid used, calculate the mass of stearic acid per drop. Show your work.

Volume = _____ cm^3

Dividing the volume by the area of the drop will give you the thickness, which is approximately equal to the molecule's length. Therefore, determine the thickness of your monolayer.

Assuming that the molecule is cubic in shape, what is the volume of the molecules?

The number of molecules can be determined by finding the ratio of the volume of stearic acid per drop to the volume of the molecules determined previously.

The number of moles of stearic acid per drop is determined by dividing the mass of the stearic acid per drop by the molecular weight of the acid (284 g/mol).

Avogadro's Number is the number of molecules per mole. The accepted value is 6.0221 × 10^{23} molecules/mole.

How many molecules per mole did you determine? (Answers of 10^{22} to 10^{23} are very much within the limits of experimental error.)

Part Five

1. Calculate the four densities (stone and three liquids).
2. Is your prediction consistent with your calculations?
3. Report your data and results in the Data Table that follows.

Data Table for Part Five

Irregular Solid

Mass: _____   Volume: _____   Density: _____

Liquid A:	**Liquid B:**	**Liquid C:**
Mass A: _____	Mass B: _____	Mass C: _____
Volume A: _____	Volume B: _____	Volume C: _____
Density A: _____	Density B: _____	Density C: _____

Show your work.

Order of liquids from bottom to top: _____, _____, _____

Is the order obtained from the observation consistent with that predicted from the calculations? _____

Why or why not?

CHAPTER FOUR

Speed, Velocity, and Acceleration

PURPOSE

In this investigation, you will experimentally determine the quantitative values of speed, velocity, and acceleration for an object in motion. The object studied will be a toy car with a student-made drip-timer attached. The scientific and mathematical concepts used in this activity are direct measurements of distance and time, along with the derived measurements of speed, momentum, motion, velocity, acceleration, force, momentum, kinetic energy, centripetal force, and potential energy.

FOUNDATIONS

Since about the fifth century BC, mathematicians were concerned with how to measure instant speed. Both Aristotle and Galileo studied and wrote about motion. Galileo was first to demonstrate acceleration when he performed his famous inclined plane experiment. This experiment was replicated by a group of students from Rice University in Houston, Texas, in 1995. Newton, in the seventeenth century, made it acceptable to measure speed over small intervals containing the instant. **Motion** is defined as the act or process of changing position and can be measured by speed, velocity, and acceleration. The definitions concerning velocity and speed follow.

The **average velocity** of an object over the interval $a < t < b$ is the net change in position during the interval divided by the change in time, $b - a$. Velocity has a direction and is measured in distance/time units, making it a vector quantity. The average velocity can be mathematically expressed as follows:

Average velocity = (Distance moved, length)/(Time elapsed)

$$v = \frac{\Delta \text{dist}}{\Delta t}$$

In SI measurements, distance is reported in meters (m), and time is given in seconds (s). Therefore, velocity is reported in meters per second (m/s). The average velocity over any interval is the slope of the line joining the points on the graph of $s(t)$ corresponding to the endpoints of the interval.

The **speed** is the magnitude of the velocity (a scalar quantity) and is always positive or zero. Speed is also measured in distance/time units.

The **instantaneous velocity** (or the **rate** at which an object is moving) at time (t) is given by the limit of the average velocity over the interval as the interval shrinks around t. The instantaneous velocity is the slope of the curve at a point.

In calculus, we call this instantaneous velocity the derivative, which is an instantaneous rate of change.

You can use your calculator to examine derivatives of a function. For example, if $f(x) = -16x^2 + 48x + 96$, then we can find the instantaneous rate of change at any given value. This can be done two ways. If you are graphing the function and already have it in Y1, then you can simply use the command shown in Figure 4.1:

```
nDeriv(Y₁,X,3)
                -48
```

Let's talk about the syntax used in this command. The command nDeriv is an abbreviation for numerical derivative. It tells the calculator to evaluate the derivative of a function at a given point. You must tell the calculator what function you want to use (Y1), you must tell it which variable you want to evaluate at (X), and you must tell it which value of X to use (3). Once you give the calculator all this information, it will display the answer to the problem. Notice that you *must* have an understanding of what you want to know in order to use this feature of the calculator. As with all calculator functions, you must be able to understand the mathematics you are asking about in order to use the calculator properly and understand the answer that it gives you.

The second way to do this problem is similar to the first. However, if you do not have the function in Y1, you can type it directly into your home screen command line using the same syntax as in the previous method (Figure 4.2).

```
nDeriv(-16X²+48X
+96,X,3)
                -48
```

FIGURE 4.2

The **acceleration** is a change of velocity (final velocity – initial velocity, $v_f - v_i$) over a unit of time and is measured in distance/time^2.

$$a = \frac{\Delta v}{t} = \frac{v_f - v_i}{t}$$

The **instantaneous acceleration** is the acceleration at some specific instant. Because velocity is reported in meters per second and acceleration is the change of velocity over time, acceleration is reported in terms of meters per second per second, or m/s^2.

$$m/s/s = \frac{\frac{m}{s}}{s} = \frac{m}{s} \cdot \frac{1}{s} = \frac{m}{s^2}$$

In calculus, we call this instantaneous acceleration the second derivative. Because acceleration also has both magnitude and direction, it is like velocity and is referred to as a vector.

To see a graphical representation of the function, the derivative, and the second derivative, you can enter each into Y1, Y2, and Y3, respectively (Figures 4.3 and 4.4). This requires that you calculate the derivatives to put them into the calculator.

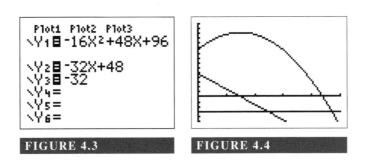

FIGURE 4.3   FIGURE 4.4

The **force** is a push or pull that can change the motion of an object and is a vector, because it is the product of mass and acceleration.

$$F = ma$$

If the mass is reported in kg and acceleration in m/s^2, then force is reported in kg·m/s^2, commonly referred to as a newton, N.

Motion is a change of position. Both force and mass influence the change of motion.

Momentum, p, is the ability to retain movement against a retarding force.

$$p = mv$$

The greater the mass, the larger the momentum (i.e., there is a direct relationship between p and m). An object's **kinetic energy,** KE, is not only related to the temperature but also to its mass and velocity. The hotter something is, the faster it moves or the greater its velocity.

$$KE = \frac{1}{2}mv^2$$

Centripetal force pulls an object out of a straight-line path into a circular path. The magnitude of the centripetal force depends on its mass, velocity, and radius, r.

$$F = \frac{mv^2}{r}$$

When an object is not in motion, we refer to its stored energy as **potential energy,** PE. PE is defined as the product of the object's mass (m), the acceleration due to Earth's gravity (g), and the height (h) the object is above the ground.

$$PE = mgh$$

Newton's Law of Gravitation is expressed by the following relationship:

$$F = G\frac{m_1 m_2}{d^2}$$

where G is identified as the universal gravitation constant, $G = 6.67 \times 10^{-11}$ N·m²/kg², and d is the distance between the two objects. As defined by this equation, the farther apart two objects are, the smaller the force between them. There is no single isolated force; all objects in the universe are attracted by all other objects in the universe. The larger the two masses are, the stronger the force is between them. If you have a ball on a small planet and then take it to another planet with a mass four times as large and a radius twice as long, how would the weight of the object differ? Remember that mass remains constant (a fundamental measurement), but weight varies by location due to the pull of gravity. In other words, mass is independent of gravity whereas weight depends on the effect of gravity. However, in the case just described, on this larger planet, if $m_2 = 4m_1$ and the distance (radius of the planet) between the ball and its surface is now $2d$, Newton's equation gives us:

$$F = \frac{Gm_1 4m_1}{(2d)^2} = \frac{Gm_1 m_2}{d^2}.$$

In other words, the effect of increased mass and distance exactly cancels, leaving the weight of the object unaffected.

Examples

1. The sun is a distance of 1.5×10^8 km from Earth. If light travels at a constant rate, c $= 3.0 \times 10^8$ m/s, how long will it take the light to reach us?
   a. One way to solve this problem is to use dimensional analysis. You are looking for a time and the only factor having anything to do with time is the speed of light. Therefore, use this factor as the first entry into the set up. You have two expressions for length, so you will have to convert m to km. (The "per s" indicated by denominator of the speed of light is considered to be exact, and therefore does not aid in determining the number of significant digits! Therefore, the number

of significant digits for the solution to this problem is two, as indicated by the distance measurement.)

$$\frac{1 \text{ s}}{3.00 \times 10^8 \text{ m}} \left| \frac{1000 \text{ m}}{1 \text{ km}} \right| \frac{1.5 \times 10^8 \text{ km}}{} = 500 \text{ s} = 5\overline{0}0 \text{ s}$$

b. Another method for solving this problem is the following. Because the expression for distance is the product of rate and time:

$$t = \frac{\text{dist}}{\text{rate}}$$

$$= \frac{1.5 \times 10^8 \text{ km}}{3.00 \times 10^8 \text{ m/s}} \left| \frac{1000 \text{ m}}{1 \text{ km}} \right| = 500 \text{ s} = 5\overline{0}0 \text{ s}$$

2. What is the acceleration of a car that moves from a speed of 10.0 m/s to that of 15 m/s over a span of time of 5.0 s?

$$a = \frac{\Delta v}{t} = \frac{v_f - v_i}{t}$$

$$= \frac{15 \text{ m/s} - 10.0 \text{ m/s}}{5.0 \text{ s}} = \frac{5 \text{ m/s}}{5.0 \text{ s}} = 1 \text{ m/s}^2$$

3. Now, let's go to the moon and repeat some of Galileo's experiments. The moon is a smaller celestial body than the Earth, so its gravitational pull is less than that of the Earth. If you have a 60.0 lb object on the Earth, it would weigh about one-sixth of that on the moon, or 10.0 lb. From the top of a 10.0 m tower located on the moon drop a ball. Every second, record the distance that the ball has fallen (see the chart that follows.) Calculate the average velocity during the first, second, and third seconds.

Time	Distance Fallen
0.0 s	0.0 m
1.0 s	0.8 m
2.0 s	3.2 m
3.0 s	7.2 m

Use the formula $v = \frac{\Delta \text{dist}}{\Delta t}$ to calculate velocity.

Time	Distance Fallen	Velocity (m/s)
0.0 s	0.0 m	*undefined*
1.0 s	0.8 m	0.8
2.0 s	3.2 m	1.6
3.0 s	7.2 m	2.4

Is velocity constant? No, it changes each second of the fall from the top of the tower.

4. Now calculate the acceleration between each second: $a = \Delta v/t$.

Time (s)	Distance (m)	Velocity (m/s)	Acceleration (m/s²)
0.0	0.0	*undefined*	
1.0	0.8	0.8	0.8
2.0	3.2	1.6	0.8
3.0	7.2	2.4	0.8

Is acceleration constant? Yes. In each case the acceleration was determined to be 0.8 m/s².

5. What force is causing this acceleration? The moon's gravity is responsible.
6. Whereas the pull of Earth's gravity is 9.8 m/s², the gravitational pull on the moon is only 1.63 m/s². The pull of Mars's gravitational force is 3.93 m/s². What can you predict about the size of Mars relative to that of the Earth and the moon?

   The size of Mars is in between that of the Earth and the moon; it has a smaller mass than the Earth and a larger mass than the moon.

Isaac Newton was a physicist who studied relationships between objects and their motion. Briefly stated, **Newton's Laws of Motion** are:

First Law: A body at rest remains at rest until acted on by a force causing it to either change its motion or alter its shape; a body in motion will remain so until acted on by a force that either changes its motion or alters its shape.

Second Law: The acceleration of an object is directly proportional to the net force acting on it and inversely proportional to its mass: $a = F/m$. More commonly this law is stated as $F = ma$.

Third Law: For every action there is an equal and opposite reaction.

A body's **inertia** is the amount of resistance to a change in its motion. A heavy mass has a greater inertia than a light one because more force must be added to change its motion or alter its shape, but after the heavy object gets moving it again will resist a change in that movement and be harder to stop. If you are traveling in an automobile at 75 mph and slam on the breaks, your car will stop but you keep going because of your resistance to the change in flow due to your inertia. Failure to properly buckle up will allow the windshield of your car to alter your motion or change your shape!

There are three parts to the activity in this investigation. The first part involves determining the speed of a toy car. The second involves constant speed, and the third involves acceleration.

INVESTIGATION

Materials

For each group

meter stick

battery-operated toy car

free-wheeling toy car

timer

masking tape

pull-type bottle cap

food coloring

medicine dropper

paper towels

two old books or something to put under table legs

Part One: Determining Average Speed

Procedure

1. Measure a 2.5 m track. Put tape at the beginning, end, and 0.5 m from the start.
2. Time the car from the 0.5-m mark to the end. Do this three times and record the data. Remember each distance moved will be 2 m.

	Trial 1	Trial 2	Trial 3
Time (s)			
Speed = distance (m)/time (s)			

3. What is the average speed?

4. Convert the average speed to cm/s and to mph. (1 m = 100 cm; 1 in. = 2.54 cm; 1 ft = 12 in.; 1 mi = 5280 ft; 1 hr = 60 min; 1 min = 60 s)

Part Two: Determining Constant Speed

Procedure

1. The first step is to determine the drip-rate for the bottle cap. Fill the bottle cap with water. Open the top until it drips at about 2 to 3 drops per second. Be sure the drops are constant at about that rate.

2. Determine how long it takes to drip 10 drops three different times and take the average.

Trial 1 time = _____   Trial 2 time = _____   Trial 3 time = _____

Average 10 drops trial time = _____

3. Calculate the average number of drops per second.

Average drops per second = _____

4. Tape the bottle cap timer to the car. Make sure it is in the middle of the back.

5. Put food coloring in water used to fill bottle cap. Be sure to keep your finger over the dripper and *do not move the dripper.* If you move the dripper, you have to repeat steps 1–3.

6. Use the same track from Part One, but put paper towels along the length of the track.

7. Turn the car on and let it move along the track. Observe the pattern of drops of colored water. Describe the pattern.

8. Measure the distances between the colored drops to nearest 0.1 cm, beginning with the third drop. Measure front to front and record in the chart provided.

9. Replace the paper towels or change the water's color and repeat two more times.

Drops	Trial 1	Trial 2	Trial 3	Average distance
3 & 4				
4 & 5				
5 & 6				
6 & 7				
7 & 8				
8 & 9				
9 & 10				

10. Does the car travel the same distance between drops?

11. Complete the following table:

End drop	4	5	6	7	8	9	10
Total distance							

12. Graph the scatterplot of the data from step 11, letting drops be the *x*-axis.

13. What does the graph appear to be?

14. Calculate the best-fit regression equation and explain in terms of the investigation what *a* and *b* (displayed on your calculator) mean.

Part Three: Determining Acceleration

Procedure

    1. In this part, we will determine acceleration of a freewheeling toy car. Place the freewheeling car with the bottle cap attached on a table or board. Lift one end of the table or board until the car starts to move. Be sure the drips have been calibrated.

    2. Place paper towels on the table or board then let the car move from the top to the bottom. Be sure the drops are about 2–3 per second (recalibrate dripper, if necessary).

3. Describe the placement of the water drops.

4. Replace the paper towels or change the water's color and repeat two more times. Record the distances between drops in the chart provided.

Drops	Trial 1	Trial 2	Trial 3	Average Distance
3 & 4				
4 & 5				
5 & 6				
6 & 7				
7 & 8				
8 & 9				
9 & 10				

5. Does the car travel the same distance during each time interval? How can you tell?

6. Complete the following table:

End drop	4	5	6	7	8	9	10
Total distance							

7. Graph the scatterplot of the data from step 6 using the drops on the *x*-axis.

8. What does the graph appear to be?

9. Calculate the best-fit regression equation and explain in terms of the investigation what a, b, and c (displayed on your calculator) mean.

10. What have you discovered about the acceleration of the car as it moves down the ramp?

11. If you are a calculus student, these investigations can be extended.
   a. Find the derivative of the linear equation from Part Two and explain what it means in terms of the problem.

   b. Find the derivative of the quadratic equation from Part Three and explain what it means in terms of the problem.

   c. Turn on the derivative feature of your calculator. Investigate the values for the two curves and discuss them.

   d. What is your reaction time? Have someone hold a meter stick vertically from the top while you position your thumb and index finger at the 50.-cm mark. Your friend will drop the stick (unannounced), and you will catch it with your thumb and finger. Measure how far the stick drops. Use this distance in the equation

   $$t = \sqrt{\frac{2d}{g}}$$

to calculate your reaction time. The acceleration due to Earth's gravity, g, is the constant 9.8 m/s^2.

REFLECTIONS AND EXTENSIONS

A cantaloupe is thrown high in the air at $t = 0$ s. The chart of the path is as follows:

t (s)	0	1	2	3	4	5	6
d (ft)	6	90	142	162	150	106	30

1. Graph this on your calculator as a scatterplot and sketch the graph.

2. What type of equation does the graph appear to be?

3. Use your calculator to find the model of this equation. What is the model?

4. Compute the average velocity of the cantaloupe over the interval $4 < t < 5$. What is the significance of the sign preceding the magnitude?

5. What is the average speed of the cantaloupe over the interval $4 < t < 5$?

6. Compute the average velocity over the interval $1 < t < 3$.

7. Use the table feature of the calculator to find the distances for $t = 0.9$ and $t = 1.1$.

8. Compute the average velocity of the cantaloupe from $0.9 < t < 1.1$.

9. Compute the instantaneous velocity at $t = 1$.

10. When does the cantaloupe hit the ground?

11. When does the velocity equal zero?

12. What is the potential energy of the cantaloupe as it rests on the ground?

13. What can you say about the acceleration of the cantaloupe after you compute it?

14. Given $G = 6.67 \times 10^{-8}$ dynes·cm^2/g^2 (a dyne is a unit of force in the English system of measurement), compute the mass of the Earth, m_E. The Earth will attract a 1.00 g mass at its surface with a force of approximately 980 dynes. If this 1.00 g object rests on the Earth's surface, the distance between the centers of both masses is approximately the radius of the Earth, 6.38×10^8 cm. Calculate the density of the Earth.

15. As mentioned previously, Galileo conducted his famous inclined plane experiment where he discovered the concept of acceleration. He used a smooth wooden plank about 7-m long with a channel cut in it about as wide as a finger. He rolled a smooth round bronze ball down this incline. He used a water clock to measure time and collected his data for time in terms of mL of water, and distance was one-quarter, one-half, and three-fourths of the length of the plank. This experiment was replicated and the data follow:

Time (mL water)	0	23.5	40.0	52.0	62.0	72.0	84.0	90.0
Distance (m)	0	0.301	0.914	1.52	2.13	3.05	3.96	4.57

a. Plot this data on the graphing calculator, letting the x-axis be time, then sketch the plot.

b. Use the regression feature of the calculator to find the quadratic equation. What is the equation?

c. If the length of the plank is 4.60 m, use the regression equation to find what the mL of water would be for one-fourth, one-half, and three-fourth the lengths will be. Write these three ordered pairs.

d. Galileo discovered that the time and distance traveled were related. Use the three ordered pairs from part c to see what Galileo discovered.

e. How does this discovery relate to acceleration?

f. Use calculus to find the velocity and acceleration for this experiment.

g. Do the results from part f relate to parts d and e? How?

CHAPTER FIVE

Heat and Temperature

PURPOSE

This open-ended investigation allows you to develop your own procedure for determining how to calibrate a thermometer in degrees Celsius. The only instruction given is to obtain the temperature of a glass of tap water with their uncalibrated thermometers. At the completion of the inquiry, class data are obtained to calculate the statistics. Next, you will compare your experimental value to the true value for the purpose of calculating a percentage error and develop a heating curve for water. The mathematical, scientific, and statistical concepts used in this experiment are temperature measurement, scale, measures of central tendency, measures of deviation, percent, absolute value, graphing functions, and the conversion between degrees Celsius and degrees Fahrenheit. A temperature probe with a graphing calculator or computer can also be used to collect the data in Part Two.

FOUNDATIONS

This investigation starts with the basic science concepts of energy (heat) and the measurement of heat intensity (temperature), and integrates the mathematical and statistical concepts of scale, measures of central tendency and dispersion, inverses, and regression. The biological aspects of conversion of food energy to heat units (calories) can be demonstrated by the classic combustion of high-sugar-content candy in melted potassium chlorate. In this investigation, the validity of the experiment can be evaluated using the concepts of percentage error and standard deviation and a regression line can also be calculated. Graphing is an important technique that allows you to better understand the collected data and to view data on a more conceptual basis.

Science Foundation

Common uses of words *heat* and *temperature* allow us to interchange them in our vocabulary frequently, but these words actually have different meanings. **Heat** is a quantity of energy due to the motion of particles. **Temperature** is said to be a measure of the intensity of the heat. Temperature is a fundamental measurement. The standard measurement for temperature is obtained in Kelvin units. The Kelvin scale has an absolute zero. At 0 K, all molecular motion is said to cease. Often in laboratory situations, temperature is reported in degree Celsius. A thermometer based on the Celsius scale has its zero point at the freezing point of water. The Celsius scale is based on the freezing and boiling points of distilled water (i.e., 0 °C and 100 °C.) Heat, on the other hand, is a derived unit. By the use of the following mathematical relationship, you can calculate the heat associated with a temperature change for a substance:

$$H = sm (\Delta T)$$

or

$$Q = sm (\Delta T)$$

To determine heat, H or Q, multiply the mass, m, of the substance by the change of temperature of that substance, ΔT, and next multiply by the specific heat capacity of the substance, s. Specific heats are reported in terms of calories (or Joules) of energy per gram degree Celsius (or Kelvin), cal/g °C. The magnitude of one degree Celsius or one unit Kelvin is exactly the same. Because we deal with the difference between the starting and final temperatures of a substance, the reporting between °C and K scale is inconsequential. Heat is usually measured in terms of calories or Joules. (1.00 cal = 4.184 J)

Units of heat that are associated with the energy content of food and its conversion into a usable form are labeled *calories*. Food calories and calories are related in that 1 Cal = 1000 cal or 1 kcal. When we say that a piece of candy has 12 Cal, we are actually talking about 12,000 cal! This means that if the piece of candy were to be completely burned (converted to energy), it would produce 12 kcal of heat.

Mathematics and Technology Foundation

There is a linear relationship between Fahrenheit and Celsius temperatures. The conversion equation can be written as

$$°F = \frac{9}{5} °C + 32$$

or

$$°C = \frac{5}{9} (°F - 32).$$

The respective equations for conversions adjust for the fact that the Fahrenheit and Celsius temperatures have different sized units and different zero points. Mathematically, these two equations are inverses of each other. This can be verified by composing the functions or by solving for an inverse.

To confirm either or both of these equations and to prepare for the technology needed in the investigation, enter temperature data into L1 and L2 of your graphing calculator's STAT feature (Figures 5.1, 5.2, and 5.3). Notice the equation obtained uses °C as the independent variable and °F as the dependent variable. To verify the other conversion equation, simply interchange L1 and L2 in the regression command and perform the calculation again (Figures 5.4 and 5.5).

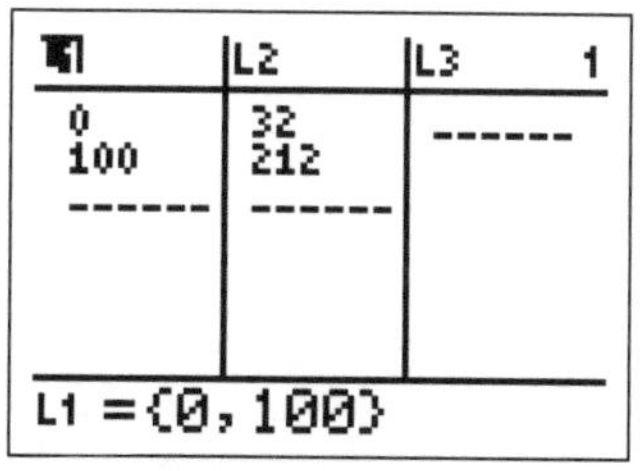

FIGURE 5.1

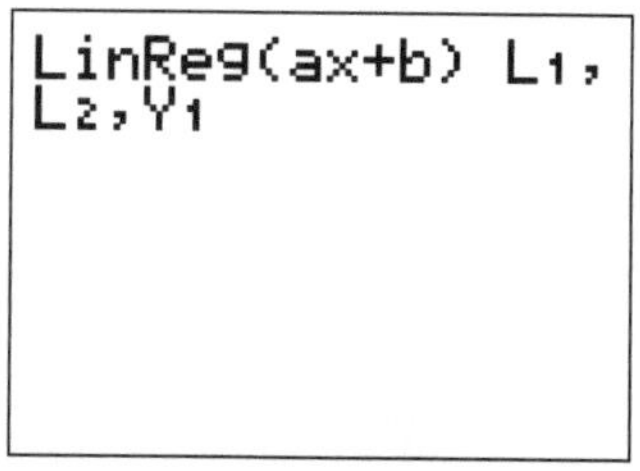

FIGURE 5.2

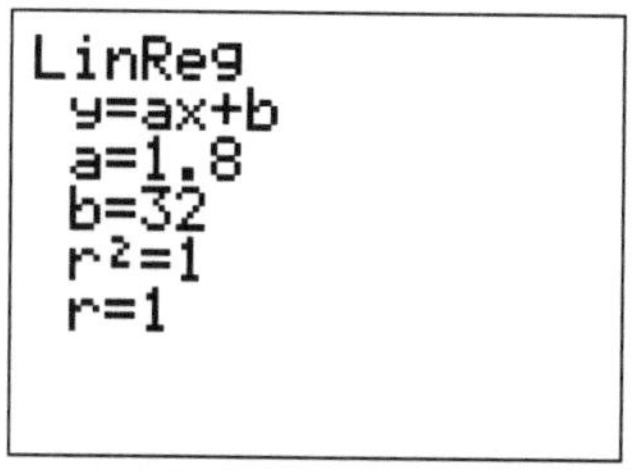

FIGURE 5.3

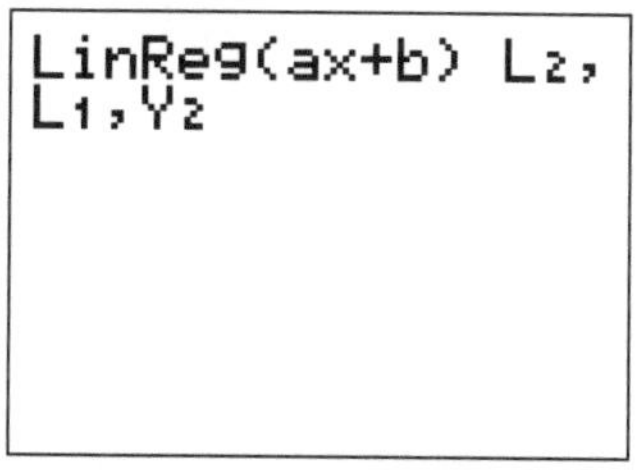

FIGURE 5.4

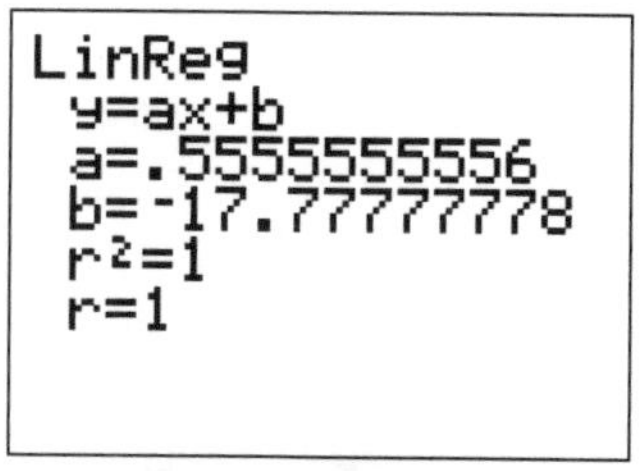

FIGURE 5.5

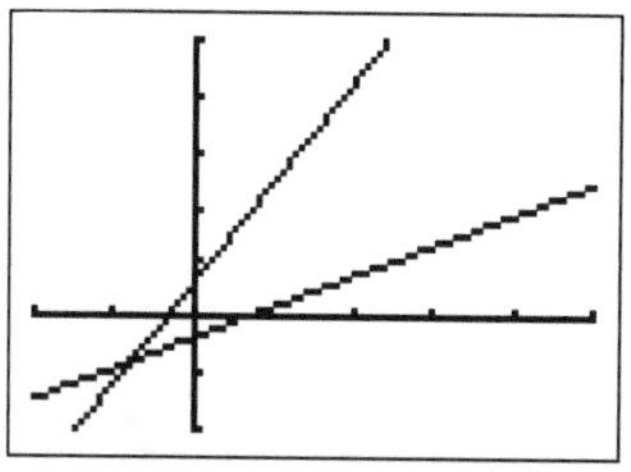

FIGURE 5.6

This equation shows the relationship when °F is the independent variable and °C is the dependent variable. The graph in Figure 5.6 shows that the two equations are inverses of each other, as is the case when dependent and independent variables are interchanged. Careful attention should always be paid to dependent and independent variables. These two concepts will play an important role in the analysis of data in this investigation. Note that the two graphs intersect at –40.0 (–40.0 °C = –40.0 °F), which can be used as a reference point. Also, note that a 100-degree change on the Celsius scale is not equivalent to a 100-degree change on the Fahrenheit scale.

INVESTIGATION

Materials

For each group

1 blank thermometer per student group

1 150-mL beaker filled with ice and distilled water (or cold tap water)

1 hot plate

beaker of ice and water

10" strip of adhesive tape from tape dispenser (place on the blank thermometer lengthwise)

1 marking pen or pencil

1 graphing calculator per person

1 metric ruler

1 ice cube, frozen with calibrated Fahrenheit thermometer or temperature probe inside the cube

Per class

1 beaker half-full of distilled water (or tap water if distilled water is not available)

1 calibrated Fahrenheit thermometer

Part One: Calibration

Procedure

1. Determine the temperature of a glass of water at room temperature by calibrating an unmarked thermometer in degrees Celsius. (You may wish to place the 10-in. tape strip on the thermometer before you begin the investigation.)
2. Put the temperature you obtained on the board, so that all laboratory groups have access to the data. (It is a good idea to estimate the temperature to the tenth's place.)
3. Calculate the mean and median of the class data gathered, using the graphing calculator.
4. Calculate the standard deviation for the class data, using the graphing calculator.
5. Obtain the temperature of the water using a thermometer calibrated in °F. Convert the temperature you measured on your calibrated thermometer in °C to °F.
6. Calculate the percentage error for your temperature. Use the mean of the class data, in °C converted to °F, as the experimental value and the temperature you measured directly in °F for the "true" value. (Percentage error is equal to the absolute value of the difference between the true (expected) value and the experimental value divided by the true value times 100.)

$$\left| \frac{\text{Expected value} - \text{Experimental value}}{\text{Expected value}} \right| \times 100 = \text{Percentage error}$$

Data Table for Part One

Temperature of water obtained in °C	
Mean temperature of class data	
Median temperature of class data	
Standard deviation of class data	
Converted temperature °F	
Percentage error	

Part Two: Heating Curve

Procedure

1. Obtain a thermometer frozen inside an ice cube (or a temperature probe frozen inside an ice cube) and a hot plate set at 7 or higher.
2. Put the ice cube/thermometer (probe) inside a small beaker and heat.

3. Collect and record data every 1 minute until the water is boiling.
4. Plot the heating curve by hand on Graph One. Plot time on the *x*-axis and temperature on the *y*-axis.
5. If a probe was not used, enter your data into a graphing calculator. Use the same *x*-axis and *y*-axis instructions as in step 4.

Graph One: Heating Curve

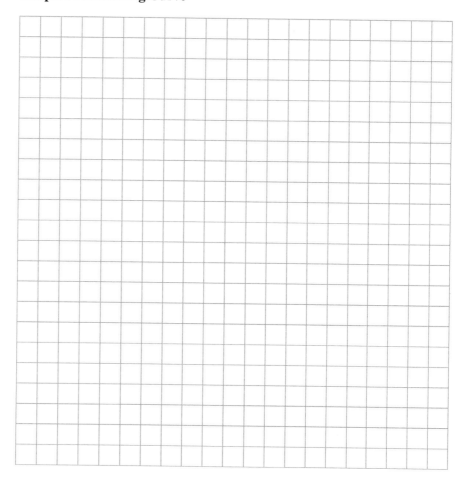

REFLECTIONS AND EXTENSIONS

1. What are the advantages of collecting a large number of data points for the same experimental value?

2. What is the meaning of a large standard deviation?

3. What are some possible sources of error in this investigation?

4. What conclusion can you draw from looking at your data for a melting ice cube? Would you expect the same phenomenon to occur during the boiling phase?

5. Use the data you gathered for the heating curve and draw a cooling curve by hand on Graph Two. Check your answer by plotting the graph on the calculator.

6. How many calories of heat would be required to raise the temperature of 50.0 g of water from 0 °C to 35 °C? (Specific heat capacity of water is 1.00 cal/g °C.)

7. The heat necessary to melt the ice is called the *heat of fusion*. Do you think that the heat (energy) needed to completely vaporize water to steam is greater or less than the heat required to melt ice? Why?

Graph Two: Cooling Curve

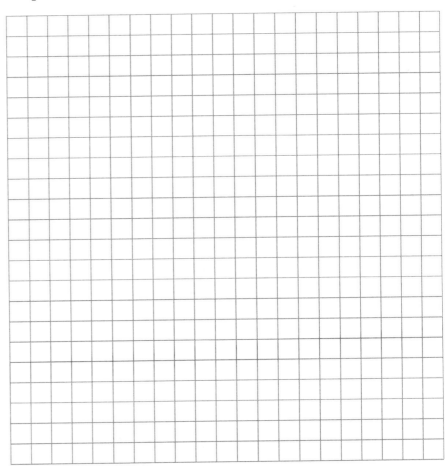

Atmospheric Heating

PURPOSE

In this investigation, you will explore the relationship of the various factors of atmospheric heating. Atmospheric heating is a major factor in determining weather and climate. There are four parts to this chapter. In Part One, you will determine the relationship of the angle of the sun to the surface area covered by the radiation. Part Two will investigate the relationship of the angle of the sun's rays and light intensity; Part Three will investigate the effect of color on albedo and heating; and Part Four will investigate the differential heating of land and water.

FOUNDATIONS

Science Foundation

Above the Earth's atmosphere, essentially nothing interferes with the solar energy streaming earthward. The solar constant is the rate at which radiant energy from the sun is received on a surface at the outer edge of the atmosphere perpendicular to the sun's rays when the Earth is at an average distance from the sun. Recent measurements taken from a satellite suggest the solar constant is 1.97 cal/cm^2/min, or 2 langleys per minute. The standard unit of solar radiation is the **langley,** equal to one calorie per square centimeter. Once the solar energy enters the atmosphere, it is no longer uniformly distributed. As the solar energy passes through the atmosphere, it undergoes absorption, reflection, and scattering. Therefore, at one location, less radiation reaches the surface of the Earth than was originally intercepted at the upper atmosphere. If solar energy were evenly distributed over the Earth's surface, our planet would have more uniform temperatures. This unequal heating drives the ocean's currents and creates the winds, which transport heat from the tropics to the poles. Energy from the sun is the important control of our weather and climate.

Weather is the state of the atmosphere at a place for a short period of time. **Climate** is a generalization of the weather conditions of a place over a long period of time. The condition of the atmosphere at any place and time is described by measuring the four basic elements of weather: temperature, moisture, air pressure, and wind. The amount of solar radiation received at any location is most responsible for causing variations in the weather elements. The principal causes of variations of solar energy reaching Earth are variations in the sun's angle, light intensity, and exposure time or duration. The seasonal variation in the angle of the sun's rays affects the amount of energy received at Earth's surface. When the sun is high in the sky, the solar rays are more concentrated and more intense. The lower the angle of the sun, the more spread out and less intense is the solar radiation.

The angle of the sun also affects the amount of atmosphere the rays must penetrate. When the sun is at 90°, or directly overhead, the rays pass through a thickness of one atmosphere. Rays entering at a 30° angle travel through twice the amount of atmosphere. The longer the path, the greater are the chances for absorption, reflection, and scattering by the atmosphere. These all reduce the intensity of the sun's rays at the Earth's surface. The Earth's orientation to the sun is continually changing as it travels in its orbit. Because variations in sun angle and length of daylight depend on the latitude, they determine the warm temperatures in the tropics and colder temperatures toward the poles. Seasonal temperature changes at a given latitude occur as the sun's vertical rays migrate toward and away from a place during the year. Thus, the energy reaching the Earth's surface is changing. Temperature is a measure of the intensity or average amount of energy reaching the Earth's surface.

Temperature is an important element of weather and climate because it greatly influences air pressure, wind, and the amount of moisture in the air. This determines the weather and climate of a location. Latitude is not the only control of temperature. The factors that cause temperature to vary from place to place and time to time are the controls of temperature. These are (1) differences in the receipt of solar energy (this is the greatest single cause), (2) unequal heating and cooling of land and water, (3) altitude, (4) geographic position, (5) cloud cover and albedo, and (6) ocean currents.

Albedo is the reflectivity of a substance that is usually expressed as a percentage of the radiation reflected from the surface. Because surfaces of high albedos are not efficient absorbers of radiation, they do not return much radiation to the atmosphere for heating. Light-colored surfaces and the air above them are typically cooler than dark surfaces. The extent of cloud cover affects the temperature. Cloud cover is important because many clouds have a high albedo. They reflect a significant portion of the sun's rays so that they return to space. By reducing the amount of incoming solar radiation, daytime temperatures will be lower than if the clouds are absent and the sky is clear. At night, clouds have the opposite effect. They act as a blanket, absorbing the outgoing radiation from the Earth's surface and radiating it back to the surface. Consequently, the temperature on cloudy nights is not as low as on clear nights. Clouds are not the only factor affecting albedo and affecting air temperatures. Snow- and ice-covered areas have high albedos. That is why snow is found on mountains in the summer and does not melt away.

The heating of Earth's surface determines the heating of the air above it and therefore, the weather. Different land surfaces absorb different amounts of solar energy that causes variations in the temperature of the air. The greatest difference is not between different land areas but between land and water. Land heats more rapidly and to higher temperatures than water. The land also cools more rapidly and to lower temperatures than water. (Remember from Chapter 5 when we talked about the specific heat of water. Water is one of the best substances we know of to absorb heat. It takes a long time for a pot of water to boil, but once it does it will retain this heat for a long time.) Temperature variation is greater over land than water.

Mathematics Foundation

Angles, which will be discussed in Chapter 13, play an important role in this chapter. Surface area, which is often calculated using complex formulae, will be used in the investigation, but without needing formulae. The functions you graph will be linear, quadratic, or exponential, all of which you have done before in this book.

INVESTIGATION

Part One: Relationship of the Surface Area of Solar Radiation (Light) and the Sun's Angle

Materials

> protractor
> manila folder
> graph paper
> high-intensity light such as a flashlight
> graphing calculator
> ruler

Procedure

1. Conduct this investigation with a partner. Open a manila folder so that one side is on the table and the other is perpendicular to the table. On the side of the table, place a sheet of graph paper. On the other side, place a mark 10 cm from the fold. It should be perpendicular to the graph paper, and the angle is 90°. Use a protractor and ruler to place marks at the angles of 75°, 60°, 45°, 30°, and 15°.
2. Darken the room. Hold the light source at a right angle 10 cm from the graph paper. Outline the area of the beam of light on the graph paper and label it, 90°. Determine the square centimeters the rays of light covered.
3. Change the angle of the light to 75° and hold the light source 10 cm from the paper. Outline the area of the beam of light on the graph paper and label it.
4. Change the angle of the light and repeat the measurements.
5. Record the data in the Data Table for Part One and then answer the questions in Reflections and Extensions using the information in the table.

Data Table for Part One

Angle of Rays, °	Lighted Area, cm²
90°	
75°	
60°	
45°	
30°	
15°	

Part Two: Relationship of the Sun's Angle and Light Intensity

Materials

    protractor

    manila folder

    graph paper

    high-intensity light

    graphing calculator

    CBL system

    light sensor

    ruler

Procedure

1. Use the equipment set up as indicated in Part One.
2. Cut a small opening in the center of the graph paper and manila folder. Place the end of the light sensor in the hole. The end of the light sensor should be perpendicular to the graph paper and should not extend beyond the surface of the paper. Tape the light sensor in position to keep it from moving.
3. Set up the calculator and CBL for a light sensor.
4. Set up the calculator and CBL for data collection.
5. Darken the room. Hold the light source at a right angle (90°) 10 cm from the light sensor paper. Collect the data on the light intensity.
6. Change the angle of the light to 75°. Make sure the light source is 10 cm from the paper. Collect data on the light intensity. Change the angle of the light and repeat the measurements.
7. Record the data in the Data Table for Part Two and answer the questions in the Reflections and Extensions.

Data Table for Part Two

Angle of Light, °	Light Intensity, mW/cm^2
90°	
75°	
60°	
45°	
30°	
15°	

Part Three: Effect of Color on Albedo

Materials

light source (reflector and 100-W light bulb)

black and silver containers (two identical metal cans, one painted black and the other silver)

Styrofoam lids to fit the top of each container

graphing calculator

CBL system

two temperature probes or two thermometers

clock

Procedure

1. Set up the calculator and CBL for two temperature probes and two temperature calibrations.
2. Set up the calculator and CBL for data collection.
3. Insert temperature probe into each Styrofoam lid so that the probe is 5 cm below the top of the lid. Place the lids on the black and silver containers. Probe 1 will be in the black container and Probe 2 in the silver container.
4. Place the black and silver containers 15 cm away from the light source. Make sure that both containers are of equal distance from the light source and are not touching one another.
5. Press ENTER on the calculator to begin collecting data. Record the beginning temperature of each container.
6. Turn on the light and record the temperature of both containers at 30-s intervals for 10 min. When the data collection is complete, display a

graph of the temperature versus time for Probe 1, the black container. Repeat for Probe 2, silver container.

7. If temperature probes are not available, use thermometers in place of the temperature probes in the containers. Record the temperature of both containers at 30-s intervals for 10 min. Record the temperatures in the Data Table for Part Three.

Data Table for Part Three

Time(s)	Temperature (°C)	
	Black Container	Silver Container
0		
30		
60		
90		
120		
150		
180		
210		
240		
270		
300		
330		
360		
390		
420		
450		

Data Table for Part Three *(continued)*

Time(s)	Temperature (°C)	
	Black Container	**Silver Container**
480		
510		
540		
570		
600		

Part Four: Water or Land—Which Heats Faster?

Materials

    water

    sand

    light source (reflector with 100-W bulb and clamp)

    ring stand

    two 250-mL beakers

    graphing calculator

    CBL system

    two temperature probes or two thermometers

    ruler

Procedure

1. Fill one beaker with 200 mL of dry sand and the other with 200 mL of water. Place the light on the stand so it is 10 cm above the top of the two beakers.
2. Set up the calculator and CBL for two temperature probes and two temperature calibrations.
3. Set up the calculator and CBL for data collection.
4. Carefully insert Probe 1 just below the surface of the sand. Suspend Probe 2 just below the surface of the water.
5. Record the starting temperatures for both the dry sand and water.
6. Turn on the light and record the temperature at about 30-s intervals for 10 min. If temperature probes are not available, use thermometers in place of the temperature probes in the containers. Record the temperatures in the Data Table for Part Four.

Data Table for Part Four

Time(s)	Temperature (°C)	
	Sand	Water
0		
30		
60		
90		
120		
150		
180		
210		
240		
270		
300		
330		
360		
390		
420		
450		
480		
510		
540		
570		
600		

REFLECTIONS AND EXTENSIONS

Part One

1. To determine the relationship of the angle of the light rays and the surface area the light covers, plot the angle on the *x*-axis and the lighted surface area on the *y*-axis. Plot the graph.

2. When is the light more spread out and less intense, at the lower or higher angle?

3. Summarize the relationship between the area of the sun's radiation and the angle of the sun's rays.

4. Is this equation a good fit? Why or why not?

Part Two

1. To determine the relationship of the angle of the light rays and the light intensity, plot the angle on the *x*-axis and the lighted surface area on the *y*-axis. Plot the graph.

2. When is the light less intense, at the lower or higher angle?

3. Summarize the relationship between the angle of the sun's rays and light intensity.

4. What is the exponential regression equation for the data in Data Table for Part Two?

5. Is this equation a good fit? Why or why not?

6. What is the relationship of the angle of the sun's rays, surface of the light rays, and light intensity?

7. The Earth is spherical in shape, so on any given day only places located at a particular latitude receive vertical (90°) rays from the sun. As one moves north or south of this location, the sun's rays strike at a decreasing angle. What will happen to the intensity of the rays?

8. At what time of the day would the sun's rays be the most intense? Least intense? Explain.

9. During which season will the sun's rays be closer to vertical (90°)? Explain.

10. The intensity of the sun's rays affects the amount of energy received at the Earth's surface. Temperature is a measure of the energy from the sun's radiation reaching the Earth's surface. What will be the angle of the sun's rays when the energy reaching the Earth's surface is the greatest?

11. Summarize the relationship of the angle of the sun's rays, the light intensity, and the seasons and the climate.

Part Three

1. When the data collection is complete, use the calculator to plot the temperatures from the data table on a graph. Use different symbols for the points for each container.
2. What is the linear regression equation for each can?

3. Are the fits good? Explain why or why not.

4. What is the change in the temperature, $\Delta t = (t_{max} - t_{min})$ for each container?

5. What are the rates of change in degrees per second for each can and how do these relate to the equations from question 2?

6. Which container has the higher albedo?

7. Write a statement that summarizes the results of the albedo experiment.

8. If equal amounts of radiation reach the Earth's surface, over which will the air be cooler: a snow-covered surface or a dark-colored barren field? Explain in terms of what you have learned about albedo.

9. When is it wise to wear dark-colored clothing, a sunny hot day or a cloudy cold day? Explain in terms of albedo.

10. If you lived in an area of long hot summers what type of colored roof (light or dark) would be the best choice? Explain.

Part Four

1. Do you think sand or water will heat faster? Explain your prediction.

2. Use the calculator to plot the temperatures from the data table on a graph. Use different symbols for the points for each container.
3. What are the linear regression equations for sand and water? Explain whether the fits are good and justify your answer.

4. What is the rate of change per second for sand and for water? Explain how these rates of change relate to the regression equations in question 3.

5. Which container has the greater temperature change?

6. How do the abilities to change temperature differ for sand and water when they are exposed to equal amounts of radiation?

7. Write a statement that summarizes the results of the land and water experiment.

8. A substance that absorbs more heat before the temperature changes is a stronger buffer against rising and falling temperatures. Based on your results, would the day to night temperatures be greater over water or over land? Explain.

9. Describe the effect that the location, along the coast or in the middle of the continent, has on the temperature of a city, disregarding latitude.

10. Suppose that the Earth's oceans covered only 50% of the Earth's surface instead of almost 75%. What would be the effect?

CHAPTER SEVEN

Gas Laws

PURPOSE

In this investigation, you will determine the quantitative change in volume of a confined gas when it is subjected to changes in pressure and then will attempt to determine the atmospheric pressure without using a barometer. The mathematical and statistical concepts used in the activity are measurements of pressure and volume, inverse relationships, linear regression, extrapolation, and graphing.

FOUNDATIONS

Kinetic Theory

The realization that all matter was composed of particles was not an easy notion to accept. Two ancient Greeks, Democritus and Aristotle, postulated opposing viewpoints about what matter was around 400–350 BC. Aristotle is credited with stating that matter was composed of one continual substance called **hyle.** Because of his status in the ancient Greek world, his theory of matter was readily accepted along with his description of matter as a substance composed of four elements (earth, wind, fire, and water). No one successfully challenged his observation for almost 2000 years. Around the same time Aristotle posed his theory, Democritus proposed the first "atomic theory." It was not until around 1808 AD that John Dalton gathered enough experimental evidence to bring back an atomic theory. His theory had some problems because subatomic particles and isotopes were yet to be discovered, but it did add credence to what Democritus had postulated: that matter is composed of **atomos** (particles).

The kinetic theory is based on the following assumptions:

1. All matter is composed of particles.
2. The particles of matter are in constant random motion.
3. Ideally, gas particles are point masses with no attractive or repulsive forces between them.
4. Gases are easily compressed and will expand to fill the volume of their container.
5. All collisions are perfectly elastic.

When gas particles are heated, their kinetic energy (the energy a body possesses because of its motion) is increased. The average speed of the particles in the gas depends on their mass and temperature. As the temperature increases, so does the kinetic energy and in turn the velocity of the particles. An increase in kinetic energy results in an increase in the random motion and the potential of an increased number of collisions. The more times particles hit each other and the sides of the vessel that contains them, the higher the pressure becomes. To further increase the chances of collisions (i.e., increase the pressure), one may reduce the volume of the confined gas or increase the temperature.

Atmospheric pressure is used as a scientific standard of pressure. The standard is defined as the average pressure of the air at sea level under normal conditions. Of course normal conditions may be somewhat subjective, so the standard is defined in terms of conditions that can be reproduced in a laboratory: 1 atmosphere pressure (atm) at a temperature of 0 °C. There are numerous ways in which to measure pressure. The list below consists of conversion factors for pressure measurements.

At 0 °C, 1 atm of pressure is equivalent to:

760. mm Hg = 760. torr = 1.01325 bar = 1013.25 mbar = 14.7 psi = 101,325 Pa

Meteorologists in the United States report the daily atmospheric pressure in inches of mercury (in. Hg). The standard in this unit is approximately 29.9 in. Hg. Pressure is measured using an instrument called a *manometer*. A manometer that measures atmospheric pressure is called a *barometer* and a manometer that measures blood pressure is called a *sphygmomanometer*.

We are always surrounded by some amount of atmospheric pressure. This air pressure is equal in all directions. When you travel to the top of a mountain, the atmospheric pressure around you is decreased. This poses a practical problem in cooking. With less pressure in the air surrounding you, food preparation requires increased time because although it will be easier for food to reach its boiling point, the temperature will be lower than that needed to cook the food thoroughly. Consequently, you have to cook food longer at higher elevations to compensate for the lower boiling temperatures. Water may boil as low as 90 °C on Pike's Peak, so you will have to cook the food longer to compensate for this "cold" boil. Alternatively, you can increase the pressure in the cooking container and raise the boiling temperature through use of a pressure cooker.

Gas Laws

Solving gas law problems can be explained by traditional formulae, but you can also make use of mathematical relationships. As you increase the pressure on the confined gas in the syringe, the volume decreases. This phenomenon is known as an *inverse relationship*. When solving gas law problems, always try to think ahead as to what the expected outcome is when you change the variables such as pressure, temperature, and volume. When you multiply by ratios greater than one, the product increases; when you multiply by ratios less than one, the product will be less than the original. For example, if you have an initial volume of 14 L of a gas and you increase the pressure on that confined gas, you would expect the final volume to be less than the initial volume. How much less depends on the ratio between the two pressures.

Example. Consider a 1.5 L sample of a gas at a pressure of 50. torr. Next increase the pressure to 150 torr. Do you expect the volume to be more or less? You should anticipate having a smaller volume because you have greater pressure! Therefore, your decision is to either multiply the initial volume by a ratio of 50. torr/150. torr or 150. torr/50. torr. Anticipating that your volume will be less, you know that multiplying 1.5 by 1/3 will decrease the volume as opposed to multiplying by 3/1, which will result in an increased volume. Therefore:

$$\frac{1.5\,\text{L}}{}\left|\frac{50.\,\text{torr}}{150.\,\text{torr}}\right| = 0.50\,\text{L}$$

How do you think temperature changes would affect the volume of a confined gas? When a balloon gets hotter, does the volume increase or decrease? When doing gas law problems that involve temperature changes, we always have to put the temperatures in terms of Kelvin units because we must have an absolute zero point on which to base our ratios. The Kelvin scale is based on what is known as absolute zero, or theoretically, the point at which all molecular motion ceases. (To convert °C to K, add 273.)

Volume

Because we will be using soda cans in the experiment, let's look at the cans in more depth. A soda can is a right circular cylinder. The formula for the volume of a right circular cylinder is as follows:

$$V = \pi r^2 h$$

where r is radius and h is height. It is important to note that the radius and height must be in the same units. Volume is measured in units cubed or cc or mL. (*Note:* 1 cc = 1 mL = 1 cm^3.)

Example. A soda can has a radius of 6.5 cm and a height of 12.1 cm. Find the volume of the can.

$V = \pi(6.5\,\text{cm})^2(12.1\,\text{cm}) = 1606.06\,\text{cm}^3 = 1600\,\text{cm}^3$
(significant digits)

The volume formula can be graphed as a function. Notice there are three variables in the formula: volume, radius, and height. When graphing, one of these must be the independent variable, one the dependent variable, and one will have to remain constant.

Example. What is the graph of the volume function as height varies with a radius of 6.5 cm?

In this example, height is the independent variable, volume is the dependent variable, and the radius remains constant.

Enter $y = \pi(6.5)^2 x$ into the Y = screen of the calculator, as shown in Figures 7.1 and 7.2.

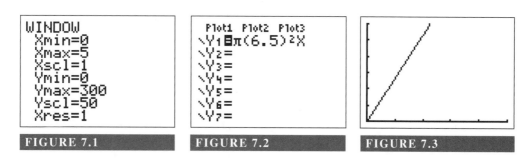

FIGURE 7.1   FIGURE 7.2   FIGURE 7.3

It can be seen in Figure 7.3 that this function is linear.

Example. What is the graph of the volume function as radius varies with a height of 12.1 cm (Figures 7.4 and 7.5)?

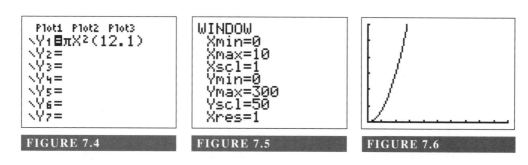

FIGURE 7.4   FIGURE 7.5   FIGURE 7.6

Here the independent variable is radius, volume is the dependent variable, and height remains constant. It can be seen in Figure 7.6 that this function is a quadratic.

Reciprocal

The reciprocal of a number is the number divided into one.

Example. Find the reciprocal of 20.

Dividing 1 by 20, we get 0.05. Any number except zero has a reciprocal. Some functions can also have reciprocals. There are functions that do not have reciprocals, such as $y = 0$.

Example. Graph the function $y = x$ and its reciprocal $y = 1/x$ (Figures 7.7 and 7.8).

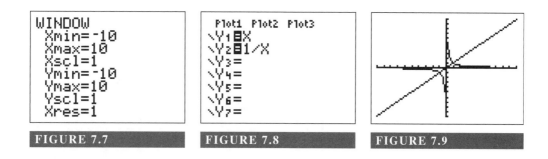

FIGURE 7.7   FIGURE 7.8   FIGURE 7.9

Notice that the reciprocal, or inverse proportion, of a function is not the same as an inverse function. This can be seen on Figure 7.9 since the functions are not reflections about the line $y = x$. Recall the inverse functions $y = 2x + 4$ and $y = (1/2)x - 2$. It can be shown that they are inverse functions by composing the functions or by looking at the graphs shown in Figures 7.10, 7.11, and 7.12.

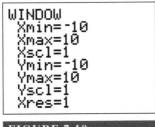

FIGURE 7.10

FIGURE 7.11

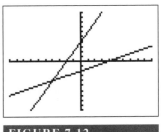

FIGURE 7.12

INVESTIGATION

Materials

For each group

1 50-cm^3 plastic syringe (capped)

6 soda cans (355 mL) (be sure to use same brand and type of soda can for each group)

graphing calculator

Procedure

1. Do this investigation with a partner. Make sure your syringe is tightly capped, and preset the syringe at the 50-cc level (always measure from the same place on the syringe's plunger). Remember, even with nothing on top of the syringe, there is still atmospheric pressure and friction holding the syringe in place; 0 cans does not represent 0 atm pressure!

2. Determine and record the gas volumes with 0, 1, 2, 3, 4, 5, and 6 cans stacked on top of the syringe. This requires carefully balancing the cans on top of each other, so be aware of how unsteady the column of cans becomes!

3. Repeat the above procedure two more times, each time resetting the syringe at the 50-cc mark.

4. Because the weight pushing on the plunger is in cans, you will first need to determine the atmospheric pressure in cans.

5. Record all data in the following table.

Number of Cans	Volume (cm³)			Average Volume (cm³)	Reciprocal Volume (cm³)	Atmospheric Pressure (no. of cans)	Total Pressure (no. of cans)	Total Pressure Times Volume
	Trial 1	Trial 2	Trial 3					

6. To determine atmospheric pressure in cans, plot on Graph One the reciprocal volume (x-axis) versus pressure in number of cans (y-axis). Draw the best-fit line among all data points. To obtain the atmospheric pressure, extrapolate the line until it intersects the y-axis. This value of y will be a negative number of cans. The absolute value of y represents the atmospheric pressure in cans (i.e., the initial pressure on the syringe before any cans of pressure were added.)

What is your value for the atmospheric pressure in cans? _____

7. Now enter the data in the graphing calculator by putting the reciprocal volumes in L1 and the number of cans (0–6) in L2. Graph the scatterplot. Be careful setting the window. Use the statistics feature to determine the linear regression equation. Graph the equation on the scatterplot. Find the y-intercept.

What is the value of the y-intercept? _____

Do you expect to have the same results as in step 6? Explain.

8. The force pushing on the syringe is the weight of the cans and the atmosphere. Because all are applied to the top of the syringe (same area), mathematically the pressure is proportional to the force. Complete the data table by multiplying the total pressure (atmospheric pressure plus the number of cans) by the average volume.

9. On Graph Two, plot the volume in cm^3 on the x-axis and the total pressure (in cans) on the y-axis.

10. Now enter the data into the graphing calculator by putting the volume into L3 and the total pressure (in cans) in L4. Graph the scatterplot, then use the regression feature to estimate the equation of the regression line.

Graph One.   Reciprocal Volume vs. Pressure in Number of Cans (label and scale x-axis from 0.00 to 0.04 and y-axis from –20 to 10)

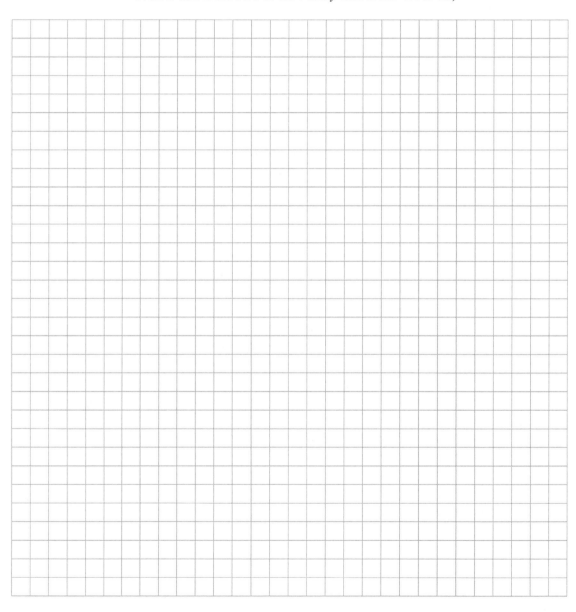

Graph Two. Volume vs. Pressure (label and scale *x*-axis from 0 to 60 cc and *y*-axis from 0 to 20 in cans)

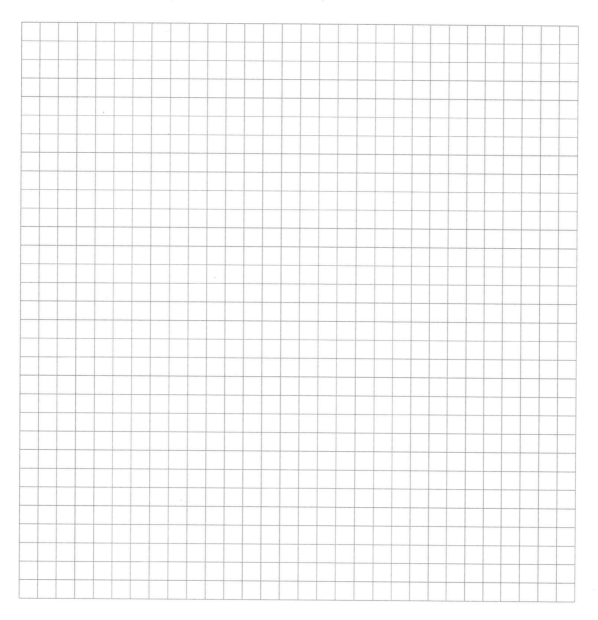

REFLECTIONS AND EXTENSIONS

1. For Graph One, what window did you enter into the calculator? For *x*? For *y*?

What would happen to the graph if you changed the *x*-window to –1 to 0.20?

2. What is the equation for your regression line?

3. What would be the total pressure if 15 cans were placed on the syringe?

4. If the total pressure doubles, what happens to the volume?

5. Look at your data table. Compare the different readings for the product of total pressure and volume. What general assumptions can you make?

6. When the pressure on a confined gas is increased, what happens to its volume?

7. A sample of neon gas occupies 15 L at 0 °C under a pressure of 1.2 atm. What volume would it occupy at 1.5 atm and 0 °C?

8. A sample of nitrogen gas occupies 12.0 L under a pressure of 790 mm Hg. At what pressure would it occupy 14.4 L, assuming constant temperature?

9. A sample of oxygen gas occupies 186 mL at 100. °C. Calculate what the volume would be if the temperature were raised to 300. °C. (Assume constant pressure.)

10. A sample of argon gas is collected at 0. °C and .98 atm. Its original volume is 2.53 L. What volume is needed when the temperature is raised to 27 °C and the pressure is lowered to 705 mm Hg?

CHAPTER EIGHT

Electricity, Magnetism, and Electromagnetism

PURPOSE

In this chapter, consideration is first given to the phenomena of electricity and magnetism individually and then to the result of their interaction: electromagnetism. Much like the philosophical idea of yin and yang, electric and magnetic fields can be viewed as two necessary expressions of a whole. The end-of-chapter explorations will compare various aspects of each of the three categories. The complexity of mathematics involved in the material addressed is limited to algebraic and trigonometric functions. Students need to be able to manipulate given formulae to solve for an unknown.

FOUNDATIONS

Science Foundation

When talking about electricity, we need to first consider energy in general. Energy is around us in many forms, and we do not usually think about where it comes from or what happens to it. However, a basic understanding of energy laws helps to connect the principles discussed in this chapter.

Energy in short is the ability to do work and is available in radiant, chemical, nuclear, kinetic, potential, thermal, and electromagnetic forms. Although we can convert energy from one of these forms to another, the total amount of energy in the universe is constant. The Law of Conservation of Energy (First Law of Thermodynamics) describes this overall constancy of energy. Although the overall energy is constant in the universe, each conversion of energy from one form to another is accompanied by a loss of (at least to us) directly usable energy. Most of the time this is thermal energy. An example is a ball being thrown up in the air. As the ball follows its path of first rising then dropping, it has a combination of kinetic and potential energy on the way up, only potential energy on the highest point of the path, and then again a mixture of kinetic and potential energy on the way down. As it lands on the ground, some of the kinetic energy is converted into elastic energy and the ball bounces up, but another part of the energy becomes thermal energy, so the ball's bounce is not going to rise to an equal elevation. As processes in a closed system (one without external inputs or outputs) such as the universe occur, a general degradation of order also occurs. This dispersion of energy is known as **entropy.** In a simple analogy this is equivalent to observing that your child's room seems to become increasingly messy over time, without anyone (least of all your child) doing anything to it.

Our experience of life on Earth seems to contradict the idea of spontaneously increasing entropy. We see plants organizing molecules of oxygen, carbon dioxide, and water into sugar molecules and know that a single molecule must be representing more order than the individual reactants. This seeming disagreement with the Law of Entropy can be easily explained if we remember that the law itself refers only to a closed system. Our Earth is an open system, with inputs and outputs to its surroundings. We can see without difficulty that the remainder of the universe more than counters the impact of life on Earth.

Electricity

The interest in electric phenomena started fairly early in human history, the earliest being the observation of lightning. Greek investigators around 600 BC found that if they rubbed amber, a hard fossilized tree sap, against fur, it would attract straw. They called what we know as amber *electron,* which laid the foundation for our use of the word today. Benjamin Franklin, one of the great American politicians, also was interested in electricity and showed experimentally that sparks that brought forth from charged amber were really the same phenomenon as lightning. Scientists around the world contributed to the better understanding of electricity and to its practical application today. To name just a few of these great scientists, Galvani and Volta of Italy, Michael Faraday and James Watt of Great Britain, Andre Marie Ampere and Charles Coulomb of France, Thomas Edison of the United States, and Georg Simon Ohm of Germany contributed greatly to the process. (See the following URL for more information on the history of electric discoveries: www.codecheck.com/pp_elect.html)

Electric charges occur in many ways in nature, such as during a thunderstorm when the charge is released by lightning. Another case of electric charges building up is when clothes are put into a dryer without adding a "noncling" product. In our childhood days, some of us may have taken delight in scraping our feet over the carpet and then touching an innocent bystander, watching a little spark zap the unfortunate soul. So, what are these charges?

An **electric charge** results when the balance of subatomic positive and negative particles is not zero, that is, when there are more of one than the other (see discussion of atoms and subatomic particles). If there is an excess of positive particles (protons), the charge will be positive, and if there is an excess of negative particles (electrons), the charge will be negative. If two objects of opposite charges are brought close enough together, they will attract each other and, as in the case of our clothes that were in the dryer without the dryer sheet, will cling. On the other hand, if two objects of like charges are brought close enough together, their charges will repel each other. An object without an initial charge may become charged by different processes that involve either transfer of electrons between objects, such as friction, or that involve a temporary separation of charges within the object, such as induction, which then can be thought of as polarization. From this we can also see that the total electric charge of the universe is constant, as there is no creation or destruction of charged particles in the process.

Because charge can be understood as a quantized entity (i.e., the number of electrons moved either between objects or within an object), it is possible to determine the charge of an object based on the **fundamental charge** on an electron:

$$e = 1.6 \times 10^{-19} \text{ Coulomb (C)}$$

This means that our measurement of electric charge can be expressed as follows:

Quantity of charge = Number of electrons × Electron charge

$$Q = ne$$

As mentioned above, objects of like charge repel and objects of opposite charges attract each other. The charged object will be surrounded by a measurable electric field that is not directly visible, but the effects of which can be directly observed and can be measured with equipment. Figure 8.1 shows field lines between two attractive and two repulsive point charges, a graphic depiction of the interaction between two charged particles.

As you can see, the lines between two attractive fields will join and exert a pull on each other; the lines between two repulsive fields will push each

Electric field lines for opposite charges

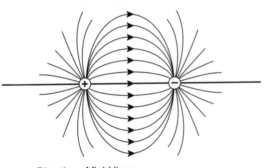

→ Direction of field lines

Electric field lines for like charges

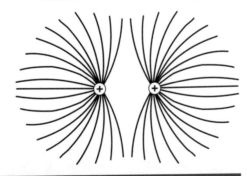

FIGURE 8.1   Interaction between Two
Charged Particles

other away. As the two charges are moved further away from each other, their influence on each other will decrease dramatically. Coulomb defined a mathematical expression that describes this interaction as follows:

$$F = k \left(\frac{q_1 q_2}{d^2} \right)$$

where F is the electric force between the charges, k is a proportionality factor with a value of 8.99×10^9 N·m²/C², q signifies an individual charge, and d is the distance between the charges. This equation became known as Coulomb's Law and shows that, as one point charge is moved away from another, the effect decreases by the square of the distance. Note the similarity to Newton's Universal Law of Gravitation:

$$F = G \left(\frac{m_1 m_2}{d^2} \right)$$

Let us now address the meaning of terms found on any electric appliance or connection in a regular household. **Electric potential** refers to the difference in potential as a charge is moved through a distance within an electric field and can be viewed as work being done on the charge. We know the basic formula for work in the sense of mechanics:

Work = Force × Distance

$W = Fd$

and can extend this relationship to our understanding of electricity:

Work = Charge on Q × Potential

where Q is the test charge itself, or the object under study. The unit of measure for potential is Joule/Coulomb (J/C), or more simply and more commonly, volts (V). Electric potential is commonly referred to as the **voltage.** What the voltage rating of an outlet or battery gives us is the potential difference between its poles, and thus a rating of the ability to do work. As a light switch is turned on or a light fixture is plugged in and turned on, a connection is made between these poles, closing a circuit, and the flow of electrons causes the light bulb to give off light. This flow of electricity is termed the **current** (I) and is measured in Coulombs/second, commonly known as Amperes (A). The formula for current is as follows:

$$\text{Current} = \frac{\text{Charge}}{\text{Time}}$$

$I = \frac{q}{t}$

As this is a flow of electrons, the movement is from areas of negative charge to areas of positive charge. Currents occur in two different ways: **direct current** (DC) flows continuously into the same direction, and **alternating current** (AC) oscillates in two opposing directions. Good sources of

DC electricity are common batteries or, and this is much more fun, items such as a balloon that may be charged by rubbing it against one's hair or with a woolen cloth. This process causes a charge build-up in the balloons so that when it is held against a wall, it will cling for a short time until an equilibrium between positive and negative charges is reestablished. AC electricity is provided by power plants, and thus any electrical connection in a standard home is supplied this way. The advantage of AC is greater efficiency, allowing transformation to higher and lower voltages and thus better distribution from the generating plant to the end user. Independently of whether electricity is supplied by an AC or DC source, if flow of electrons is to occur, a closed pathway, known as a circuit, has to exist.

Not all materials will allow electrons to flow, and not all materials that allow electrons to flow will allow them to migrate with equal ease. Different materials have different atomic make-ups, and some of those will allow the flow of electrons through the material with greater ease than others. For example, copper is an excellent material for conducting electricity because it greatly facilitates the flow of electrons in and out of vacant orbitals in the atoms' outermost energy levels. This distribution of electrons is sometimes referred to as a *sea of electrons.* Such a material is known as a good **conductor.** On the other hand, materials such as plastic or wood hinder the flow of electrons and are known as good **insulators or nonconductors.** (However, research is under way to develop new plastics with different properties. Imagine that one day we may have plastic solar cells.) The quality of a material to conduct or insulate is then due to how much resistance it puts up against electron flow and is known as **resistivity** (ρ). Just like friction in the mechanical domain, **resistance** slows electrons down, and can cause loss of energy in the form of heat. Such a loss of energy in the form of thermal energy is useful under certain circumstances, such as in the filament of a light bulb. In that case the loss of energy as heat will cause the filament to glow. Resistance is calculated according to Ohm's Law:

$$\text{Resistance} = \frac{\text{Voltage}}{\text{Current}}$$

$$R = \frac{V}{I}$$

The unit for resistance is volt/amperes (V/A), commonly known as ohms (Ω). It is interesting to note that wires with smaller diameters have higher electrical resistance. This makes sense when considering that resistance to flow, when viewed as an analog to friction, must be higher when there is more opportunity for friction as is given by a smaller diameter. In addition, the longer a wire is, the more energy loss there will be. To calculate the resistance of a given wire, consideration must be given to the resistivity of the material of the wire (ρ), the length of the wire (l) and the cross-sectional area of the wire (A). The mathematical expression then is as follows:

$$\text{Resistance of a wire} = \text{Resistivity} \left(\frac{\text{length}}{\text{Area}} \right)$$

$$R = \rho \left(\frac{l}{A} \right)$$

As different materials have different resistivities, it is of advantage to use the best conductor to supply electricity to end-users. However, the advantage in lower resistivity alone will not determine which material is the most widely used. The material also has to be economically feasible. Most wiring is done with copper wires for precisely that reason, even though silver wire has a considerably lower resistivity than copper.

Power measures how quickly work is being done, whether we are looking at mechanics or at electricity, and its unit is the watt (W). In fact, what the electricity company charges us is not measured in volts or amperes, but in kilowatt hours (kWh), the unit for **electric power.** Appliances are rated in Watts, which really are Joules of energy per second (J/s). If an appliance has a rating of 1 kW, it means that it will require 1000 J/s. If that appliance is then run for 1 hr, a total of 1 kWh is consumed, and if the power company charges $0.15 per kWh, then 15 cents will be billed for that particular usage.

Looking at electric power from the point of potential and flow, the relationship between them is as follows:

Power = Current $\times$ Voltage

$P = IV$

Let's look at an example of how power consumption is different in the United States, where in general the supplied current is 110 V, compared to Europe, where the supplied current is almost entirely 220 V. If we assume an equal flow of current, 1 A, then in the United States the power output is 110 W and in Europe it is 220 W. For the end-user, electricity is more expensive in Europe than in the United States in part due to higher taxation. Governments in Europe selected that route to encourage energy-conscious behavior—the threat of high monthly utility bills is an effective incentive to be frugal.

As already mentioned, electricity flows through closed systems. In our homes, we have to have closed loops for electricity to flow through in order to benefit from the power supplied by the electric company. These closed loops are called **circuits.** When we switch the light switch to the off position, we in fact interrupt the pathway of electron flow. One kind of circuit is wired in **series,** in which all pieces are lined up so that they are in sequence. In such a case, any interruption in the circuit will cause the flow of electricity to stop in the entire loop. For example, we may have two light bulbs connected to the same power source in such a way that they are connected one after the other on the same complete path. An example for this is a string of Christmas lights on which, when one of the bulbs burns out, none of them will be lit. On the other hand, in a **parallel circuit** there are cross-connections that will allow continued flow of electricity by a detour if one of the intermediates interrupts the path. In that case, there may be two light bulbs connected to the same power source in such a way that each has its own complete path. This can be pictured much like traffic flow in a city. If there is only one road between point A and point B, all traffic has to follow the same path, and any interruption along the way will stop all of the traffic. If, however, there is an alternate route, then some of the traffic will go either way, and in the case of an interruption along one route, flow will continue on the other.

Magnetism

Magnetism was known in ancient Greece and in early China, where certain stones, known as *lodestones,* were found to be able to attract iron. If a steel pin was rubbed repeatedly in the same direction against such a lodestone it also was able to attract iron. As early as 1000 AD, Chinese investigators found that such a pin would orient itself along the north–south axis of the Earth as long as it was freely suspended, and the compass was born (www.istp.gsfc.nasa.gov/Education/Imagnet.html).

Magnets come in many shapes and strengths. Some magnets are made to stick on refrigerators, others (strong electromagnets) can pick up entire cars, and still others give us valuable health information by magnetic resonance imaging (MRI). Lest we forget, magnets also are just plain fun to play with. Our beautiful planet itself acts like a bar magnet and creates a **magnetic field** that protects us from some solar radiation, aids migratory animals, and makes it possible to navigate with the help of a compass. Thus, much like electric charges create electric fields, magnets have magnetic fields. These magnetic fields are mathematically identified as '*B.*' The formula for magnetic field strength is as follows:

$$B = \frac{F}{q_o(v \sin \theta)}$$

where q_o is the positive test charge in the magnetic field, v is the velocity of the charge, and θ is an angle between 0 and 180° in which the charge enters the field.

By convention, **magnetic field lines** enter at the negative (south) pole and exit at the positive (north) pole. However, Earth's magnetic negative pole is actually the North Pole. The compass needle's positive north pole then is attracted to the Earth's negative magnetic pole, which is the one we refer to as the North Pole (even though, as just mentioned, it is actually what convention refers to as a south pole in any magnet). Two things need to be mentioned here: first that the Earth's magnetic poles do not quite coincide with the Earth's geographic poles, and second, Earth's magnetic field changes over time; that is, the location of the current magnetic north and south poles has not always been the same in the past and will again change in the future.

Magnetism is a fundamental force of nature, and, like gravity or electric charge, can act through space. In fact, magnetism is closely related to the properties of electric charges. As mentioned, magnets have two opposite poles, one is the north and the other the south pole. It is not possible to break a magnet into two pieces and to then end up with just one pole on each of them. Each of the smaller pieces will again have two poles. This is an important difference between magnets and electric charges. However, as is true for electric charges, magnetic poles that are opposites (i.e., one north and the other south) will attract, whereas magnetic poles that are the same (i.e., both north or both south) will repel each other. This property finds application in high-speed magnetically levitated trains. Here, the repulsion between the like poles on the train and segments of the tracks causes the train to hover just slightly above the tracks. Because there is no contact between the two, friction does not use up some of the spent energy. The train gains speed as track segments are polarized to keep pulling the train along by creating opposite poles that are switched as the train passes above the segment. The opposite sequence will slow the train down.

When two poles are brought close together, their magnetic fields will interact and behave much like the fields of two electric charges (i.e., joining between field lines if the two poles are opposite, and repulsion between the fields if they are alike). The strength of a magnetic field can be measured with the help of magnetometers, and its unit of measure is the Tesla (T).

If a **moving charge** is placed into a magnetic field so that it crosscuts the field, the field will exert a force on the charge and move it perpendicular to the direction in which the charge was moving originally and perpendicular to the magnetic field as well. Whereas the direction of movement is then changed, the speed of the moving charge is not.

To determine the magnetic field strength, where the moving charge q with a velocity v enters a magnetic field B in a direction that is perpendicular to the magnetic field, use the following equation:

$$B = \frac{F}{qv}$$

If the strength of the magnetic field is already known, it is appropriate to rearrange the formula to solve for the force (as long as the particle is still entering perpendicular to the magnetic field):

$$F = qvB$$

When the particle enters at any other angle, the formula must include the sine of that angle ($\sin \theta$):

$$F = qvB \sin \theta$$

The strength of the magnetic field (graphically depicted by the number of field lines passing through a specific area (A) that may be determined differently for different magnet shapes) is called the **magnetic flux** (ϕ) and is defined as follows:

$$\phi = BA \cos \theta$$

The unit for magnetic flux is the weber (Wb). To repeat, in a constant magnetic field, speed is constant, but direction will keep changing. The path depends on the mass of the charged particle. Mass spectrometers use this effect and help in the determination of molecular make-up: molecules under study are heated until they disintegrate into their respective fragments and are then injected into the magnetic field. The deflection of these fragments then depends on their masses and can be detected and interpreted. These instruments are widely used in chemistry, environmental science, geology, and other fields.

Another aspect of the moving charge's behavior in a magnetic field is that a wire through which current flows fulfills the same condition when placed into a magnetic field, and thus the wire itself will move. Several rules exist that help those interested to figure out direction of forces and fields in such situations. For example, the direction of the magnetic field can be determined by the "directional right-hand source rule": One simply aligns the right hand along a current-carrying wire in such a way that the thumb points into the direction of the electron flow and then curls the fingers. The curled fingers indicate the direction of the magnetic field.

Electromagnetism

The interaction between electricity and magnetism is such that each one of the partners will influence the other. Nature provides us with various examples of electromagnetism, ranging from subatomic phenomena to energy in the form of electromagnetic waves, such as visible light waves. Here waves propagate themselves even through space, without the aid of a carrying medium. The magnetic field builds the electric field, which in turn will build another magnetic field, and so on. Technologically, this interaction has been put to use in many fields.

Electromagnets are basically coils of wire wrapped around metal cores that will generate magnetic fields once a current is passed through the wire. The strength of the electromagnet is higher when there are more coils or when the current is higher.

One of the scientists interested in the interaction between a varied magnetic field in a wire loop and the induced **electromotive force (emf)** was Michael Faraday. His discoveries provide us with a principle that finds multiple applications. The electric motor, for example, uses this phenomenon: one possibility is to suspend a rotating coil of wire in which the flow direction of electrons is reversed every half-turn between stationary magnets. This then will mimic a time-varying magnetic field that continuously produces mechanical energy. The process is known as *electromagnetic induction,* as it induces the flow of electricity by magnetic field reversal. Other examples for the use of electromagnets are the generation of television pictures, speakers, and computer technology.

In the lab, induced currents are easily measured with galvanometers. A possible test sequence begins with connecting a wire loop to the instrument. As long as there is no relative movement between magnet and loop, no electric current is induced and the instrument will show a measurement of zero. However, as the magnet is moved toward and through the loop, a measurement of a nonzero value results (either positive or negative, depending on the orientation of the magnet), and movement in the opposite direction will cause a nonzero measurement in the opposite direction of the instrument's scale. As the induced current will occur as soon as there is relative movement between loop and magnet, either one can be picked up and moved to observe this effect. **Faraday's Law of Electromagnetic Induction** is a mathematical expression of this process:

$$\varepsilon = -N\frac{\Delta\phi}{\Delta t}$$

where ε is the emf, N is the number of loops in the coil, $\Delta\phi$ is the change in magnetic flux through one loop and Δt is the length of time during which the process takes place.

Mathematics and Science Connections

The following formulae will be used in the investigations. You need only basic arithmetic skills to manipulate the equations. You may want to review calculator input procedures before beginning the investigation.

Electricity Formulae

$$Q = ne \qquad F = k\left(\frac{q_1 q_2}{d^2}\right) \qquad I = \frac{q}{t}$$

$$R = \frac{V}{I} \qquad R = \rho\left(\frac{L}{A}\right) \qquad P = IV$$

$$\text{Work} = \text{Charge on } Q \times \text{Potential}$$

Magnetism Formulae

$$B = \frac{F}{q_o(v \sin\theta)} \qquad B = \frac{F}{qv} \qquad F = qvB$$

$$F = qvB \sin\theta \qquad \phi = BA\cos\theta$$

Electromagnetism Formula

$$\varepsilon = -N\frac{\Delta\phi}{\Delta t}$$

INVESTIGATION

Part One: Electricity

Materials

> one lemon (fresher is better)
> batteries: 2 AA, 1 D, 1 6-V, 1 9-V
> paper clip (metal)
> 1 m of copper wire
> 2 flashlight bulbs
> 2 bulb sockets for flashlight bulbs
> 3 pieces of copper wire with alligator clips attached at each end
> calculator and CBL with voltage probe or voltage meter
> 2 pull tabs from soda cans
> plastic comb
> woolen cloth
> sheet of notebook paper
> balloon
> permanent marker
> graphite pencil

Procedure for Static Electricity

1. Tear some of the sheet of paper into small pieces and then rub the plastic comb with a woolen cloth for about 1 min. Now bring the comb close to the bits of paper, however without touching it against the paper. Record your observations in Data Table One for Part One.

2. Blow up a balloon and rub it against your hair. Do the following (you will have to rub the balloon against your hair before each of these):

   a. Hold it near a wall and let go of it. Record your observations in the data table.

   b. Hold the balloon near paper bits. Record your observations in the data table.

   c. This activity will require students and groups to work together. With the permanent marker, make a line between the air opening and around the length of the balloon (marking two halves). Then mark one of the two halves clearly with a sign of your choice. Rub only the marked half against your hair. Lay two of these balloons on a table. First orient them so that two marked halves are directly opposing each other. Record your observations. Now lay them so that one marked and one unmarked surface are directly opposing each other. Record your observations.

Data Table One for Part One

Experiment	Observations
1	
2a	
2b	
2c	

Procedure for Batteries

1. Set up your calculator/CBL set or your voltage meter to measure electric flow.

2. *In individual turns,* test the following power sources (which are dry-cell batteries). See Figure 8.2. Record your observations in Data Table Two for Part One.

   1 AA battery

   2 AA batteries (align them so that opposite poles touch)

   1 D battery

   1 6-V battery

   1 9-V battery

   1 D battery and 1 AA battery (align them so that opposite poles touch)

   1 D battery and 2 AA batteries (align them so that opposite poles touch)

   any combination of batteries not yet tested together

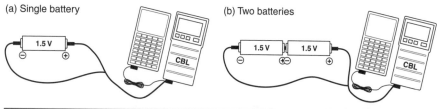

FIGURE 8.2   Testing Dry-Cell Batteries

3. Touch the end of each of your connectors to a different end of the power source (either individual or, where appropriate, systems of batteries) and measure the voltage. Record your results in Data Table Two for Part One.

4. Take the lemon and roll it under a bit of pressure on the table to free some of the juice inside—be careful not to press hard enough to break the skin. Now put a piece of copper wire (2 cm) into one side, and a straightened paperclip near it, but at least 1 cm away from the copper wire. Touch the end of each of your connectors to a different end of the power source and measure the electricity. Record your results in Data Table Two for Part One.

Data Table Two for Part One

Power Source tested	Voltage measured
1 AA battery	
2 AA batteries	
1 D battery	
1 6-V battery	
1 9-V battery	
1 D & 1 AA battery	
1 D & 2 AA batteries	
Own:	
Lemon	

5. Pick any two of the dry-cell power sources and one of the power source combinations tested above. *In separate setups,* evaluate each by using the following sequence, as illustrated in Figure 8.3. Record your observations in Data Table Three for Part One.

   a. Connect one of the light bulbs directly to a loop of copper wire attached to the battery. To do this, wrap part of the copper wire around a pull-tab from a soda can. You have to hold the bottom of the

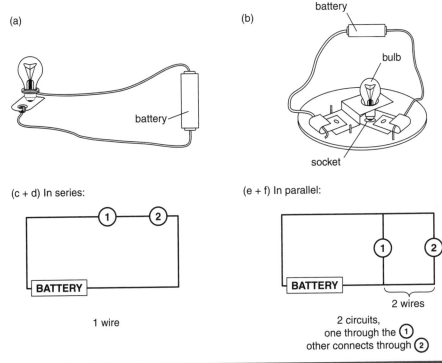

(a)

(b) battery

bulb

battery

socket

(c + d) In series:

1 wire

(e + f) In parallel:

2 wires

2 circuits,
one through the ①
other connects through ②

FIGURE 8.3   Testing Circuits

light bulb against the pull-tab setup and the side of the light bulb's metal base against the wire (it is easier if you wrap the wire around the threads of the bulb's metal base). Record your findings.

b. Remove the pull-tab and light bulb from the wire, or use a different length of wire. Connect one of the light bulb sockets to a loop of copper wire connected to the battery and put in the bulb. Record your findings.

c. Add the second light bulb in the same manner, so that they are in series, and repeat measuring the flow. Record your findings.

d. Unscrew one of the light bulbs and observe what happens. Record your findings.

e. Now change your setup so that the two bulbs are in parallel and repeat, measuring the flow. Record your findings.

f. Unscrew one of the light bulbs and observe what happens. Record your findings.

Data Table Three for Part One

Setup	Circuit tested	Observations
1	__-V battery, wire, 1 bulb	
	__-V battery, wire, 1 bulb, bulb socket	
	__-V battery, wire, 2 bulbs, 2 bulb sockets (series)	

Data Table Three for Part One *(continued)*

Setup	Circuit tested	Observations
	__-V battery, wire, 2 bulb, 2 bulb sockets (parallel)	
2	__-V battery, wire, 1 bulb	
	__-V battery, wire, 1 bulb, bulb socket	
	__-V battery, wire, 2 bulbs, 2 bulb sockets (series)	
	__-V battery, wire, 2 bulbs, 2 bulb sockets (parallel)	
3	__-V and __-V battery, wire, 1 bulb	
	__-V and __-V battery, wire, 1 bulb, bulb socket	
	__-V and __-V battery, wire, 2 bulbs, 2 bulb sockets (series)	
	__-V and __-V battery, wire, 2 bulbs, 2 bulb sockets (parallel)	

Part Two: Magnetism

Materials

2 bar magnets

horseshoe magnet

20 g dry iron filings

ZipLoc bag

paper plate

Total cereal

Procedure

1. Take a tightly sealed ZipLoc or similar bag containing iron filings and lay it on the paper plate.
2. Gently shake the paper plate to get a fairly even distribution of the filings.
3. First put only one bar magnet on the table in front of you and then carefully lower the plate onto it. Observe the pattern formed by the iron filings. Draw it into your notebook.

4. Remove the plate with the filings, and shake it again (gently) to redistribute them as evenly as possible.

5. Next put both bar magnets on the table in front of you in such a way that there is a few centimeters of distance between them. Again carefully lower the plate onto your setup. Observe the pattern formed by the iron filings, and draw it into your notebook.

6. Remove the plate with the filings, and shake it again (gently) to redistribute them as evenly as possible.

7. Now turn only one of the two bar magnets around so that its other pole faces the other of the magnets, again leaving a few centimeters of distance between them. Just as before, carefully lower the plate onto your setup. Observe the pattern formed by the iron filings, and draw it into your notebook.

8. Remove the plate with the filings, shake it again (gently) to redistribute them as evenly as possible.

9. Last, test the magnetic field line pattern you will get from a horseshoe magnet by lowering the iron filings onto it. Draw it in the notebook.

10. Take a 250-mL beaker and fill with Total cereal. Add 100 mL of water. Place a very good magnet (neodymium magnets are strong enough) underneath the beaker. Stir the mixture with a stirring rod for about 5 min. Slowly pull the magnet along the side of the beaker toward the top. Record your observations. What does it mean for a cereal to be iron fortified?

Part Three: Electromagnetism

Materials

compass

bar magnets

iron screw

1.5-m copper wire

9-V battery

calculator and CBL

Procedure

1. Wind the copper wire around the windings of the screw in such a manner that at each end at least 20 cm of wire are left. Attach the ends to the battery and then move the setup close to a compass (the copper wire/iron screw assembly has to be moved toward/over the compass). Observe what happens to the compass and record your findings in Data Table for Part Three.

2. Carefully touching the wire or battery, do you feel anything different from before you began the experiment?

3. Take the remainder of the wire and wind it into a tight coil with an inner diameter of about 5 cm, leaving at least 30 cm free at each end. Attach the ends to the connectors of your calculator/CBL setup and then hold the coils upright and tightly gathered in one hand. Now move the bar

magnet back and forth in the loop, with varying speed and stopping every now and then. Carefully observe your instrument readings and record them in your notebook. Now hold the magnet stationary and move the coil back and forth over it. Record your observations in the Data Table for Part Three:

Data Table for Part Three

Item Moved	Direction of Movement	Result

REFLECTIONS AND EXTENSIONS

Part One

1. What problems did you run into?

2. Which power supply setup worked best?

3. How did the lemon compare to an AA battery?

4. How did your results change when several batteries were lined up and tested versus each individual battery? Can you write a rule for these findings?

5. Was there a difference in how well the setup worked when the bulbs were connected to the loop without the light bulb sockets versus with the light bulb sockets?

6. Were the lights brighter in one setup than in another? If so, in which?

7. What is a major difference between serial and parallel circuits?

8. Carbon is a nonmetal. Pencil lead (graphite) is an allotrope of carbon. Is it possible for graphite to conduct electricity? Devise an experiment to prove your hypothesis and test it.

9. Measurement of the charge on a metal object shows a reading of 1.00×10^{-19} C. How many electrons are in excess on the object?

10. A 6-V battery is measured to provide 120 J of work. What is its charge?

11. An appliance requires 120 V of electricity to operate and its resistance is 600 Ω. How much power does it use?

12. A swimming pool pump with a 1500-W motor runs for 12 hours every day. For a 30-day month, how much will the electricity cost to operate this pump if the electric company charges 15 cents per kWh?

13. If two 1800 W appliances are operated on the same 120 V circuit at the same time, will a 20 A circuit breaker be tripped?

Part Two

1. What problems did you run into?

2. Which setup showed attractive forces?

3. Which setup showed repulsive forces?

4. If the strength of a magnetic field (*B*) is 2.3 T and an electron enters the field perpendicularly with a velocity of 3×10^8 m/s, how much force does the magnetic field exert on the electron?

Part Three

1. Steps one and two involved approaching a compass with a copper wire wound around an iron screw and connected to a battery. Explain your findings.

2. Step three involved interactions between a magnet and a coil of wire.

   a. What did you observe?

   b. Under what conditions did you get the greatest instrument readings?

   c. Did it make a difference whether the magnet or the coil was moved?

   d. Did it make a difference in which direction the magnet or coil was moved?

3. An electromagnet has 40 loops (N) and the change in magnetic flux has a value of 0.002 Wb over a 20. min period. What is the induced potential difference (emf = ε)?

CHAPTER NINE

Light

PURPOSE

In this investigation, you will determine the relationship of wavelength, frequency, and energy; light intensity and distance; the penetration of light waves in water and the clarity of water. The mathematical concepts used in these investigations are measurement of temperature and light intensity, inverse relationships, graphing, and exponents.

FOUNDATIONS

Science Foundation

The nature and behavior of light is different from other natural phenomena. It is not surprising that many great physicists of the past have struggled with light. Exactly what is the nature of light? Two conflicting answers to this question were proposed in the late 1600s and early 1700s. Robert Hooke and Christian Huygens argued that light travels in waves. Issac Newton considered light to be a stream of particles. According to his approach, a source of light emits tiny particles, and we are able to see objects when these tiny particles bounce off them and enter the eye. In 1801, Thomas Young, a British physicist, demonstrated that light could exhibit interference. This demonstration of interference gave the wave model of light a strong boost. Young's experiment was the first to provide a way of measuring the wavelength of light. White light is composed of all the colors ranging from red to violet. Measurements of the components of white light showed that the wavelength of red light is approximately 750 nm and that violet light has a wavelength of about 400 nm (1 nm $= 10^{-9}$ m).

Approximately 100 years after Young's experiment demonstrated the wave nature of light, a series of experiments were performed that showed that light sometimes acts as though it is composed of a stream of particles. Max Planck postulated that light coming from any source is not in the form of a continuous wave. Instead, the light is emitted in tiny bundles of energy or packets. The name for one of these discrete bundles of energy is **photon.** The energy carried by an individual photon can have only a certain value. The energy carried by a photon was determined by Planck to have a value given by the following equation:

Energy $= h \times$ Frequency of the light

$E = hv$

where h is Planck's constant, which is 6.626×10^{-34} J·s. Note that the equation indicates that the higher the frequency of the light, the higher the energy carried by a photon. Thus, the photons of violet light carry more energy than the photons of red light. Five years later, Einstein published a theory that explained the observations. In 1913, Neils Bohr developed a model of the atom that was successful in explaining how light is emitted by an atom. This model has recently been updated by what is known as *string theory*.

So what is light? Is it a wave or a series of particle-like photons? The question cannot be answered. Instead, all we can do is describe how light acts. Both descriptions are correct, light exhibits wave behavior and light acts as if it is composed of a stream of particles—wave–particle duality.

Light originates from the accelerated motion of electrons. It is an electromagnetic phenomenon and is only a tiny part of a wide range of **electromagnetic waves** called the electromagnetic spectrum. An electromagnetic wave, as its name suggests, is both electric and magnetic in nature. An electromagnetic wave consists of an electric field and a magnetic field. These fields are not made of matter but are the regions through which the push or pull of charged particles is exerted. The electric and magnetic fields are positioned at right angles to each other and in the direction of the wave motion. Unlike other waves, electromagnetic waves do not carry energy by causing matter to vibrate. It is the electric and magnetic fields that vibrate. This explains why electromagnetic waves or light can travel in a vacuum as well as through a medium.

The electromagnetic waves are arranged in order of wavelength and frequency in the **electromagnetic spectrum.** The electromagnetic spectrum ranges from long-wavelength, low-frequency radio waves to short-wavelength, high-frequency gamma rays. The electromagnetic waves that can be seen are **visible light:** red, orange, yellow, green, blue, indigo, and violet (ROY G BIV). The higher the frequency of the light, the higher is the energy carried by a photon. The greater the energy carried by a wavelength, the greater the temperature. Thus, photons of violet light carry more energy than do photons of red light. This is an extremely small portion of the electromagnetic spectrum. Despite the small range, the visible spectrum is very important. Life on Earth could not exist without visible light. Nearly half of the energy given off by the sun is in the form of visible light. Over time, organisms have evolved to utilize visible light. Visible light is essential for photosynthesis. Energy used by plants and microorganisms millions of years ago are locked up in coal and oil that is used as an energy resource today.

Because each frequency has a different amount of energy per photon, waves of different frequencies affect us and our environment in different ways. Some warm our bodies, others can kill germs, others destroy living tissue, and so forth. Sunlight, the ultimate source of most of the Earth's energy, contains a broad band of frequencies. During the day the sun is the primary source of light, and the brightness of the sky is the secondary source. Other sources are flames, white-hot filaments in light bulbs, and glowing gases in tubes.

Light waves tend to spread out as they move away from their source. The intensity decreases rapidly as the distance from the source increases. The mathematical relationship for light intensity and distance is an inverse square relationship. That is, light intensity varies inversely with the square of the distance. This is expressed mathematically as follows:

$$Y = \frac{A}{X^2}$$

where A is a constant and X is the distance.

As light penetrates water surface, passing from air to water, its intensity falls off rapidly with depth as a result of absorption and scattering. The **compensation depth** is the point below which there is no net productivity. It occurs at a water depth where light intensity is reduced to about 1% of its surface value. In clear water it can be as deep as 110 m. In sediment-laden coastal waters it is in depths of less than 20 m. The longer wavelengths of visible light, the reds and yellows, are absorbed more readily by water than the shorter wavelengths, the greens and blues. Because light intensity diminishes with depth, the water column can be divided into vertical zones. The upper zone, in which plants receive adequate levels of sunlight and can photosynthesize, is the **photic zone.** The **aphotic zone** is the zone where, due to the lack of light, plants cannot survive.

Just like plants on land, the corals in reefs depend on sunlight. The amount of light that reaches the corals is an important indicator for the purity of the water and the health of the corals. The light levels at the bottom are compared with the light coming in at the sea surface. Factors that affect how much light reaches the reefs are the time of the day, cloud cover, and the time of the year. In addition to the predictable factors, sediments or plankton in the water can affect the clarity of the water. The filtering effect of water on the light intensity can be predicted using the light extinction formula.

$$I_d = I_o e^{-kd}$$

This formula states that the intensity of light at the surface of the ocean (I_o) will decay at an exponential rate as depth (d) increases. The constant controlling this decay rate is the clarity of the water (k). When the water is very clear, k will be small; when the water contains sediments or plankton, k will be larger and less light will get through. This can be used to determine the clarity of the water and the health of the environment.

Mathematics Foundation

Exponents and the rules of exponents were discussed in Chapter 2. Those ideas play a prominent part in the mathematics background necessary for this chapter. In Chapters 5 and 7, inverse relationships were discussed. You have already seen both of these concepts demonstrated in scientific equations so far in this chapter.

INVESTIGATION

Part One: Relationship between the Distance from a Light Source and Intensity

Materials

> CBL unit
>
> graphing calculator
>
> light sensor
>
> light source (100-W bulb or flashlight)
>
> shoebox
>
> meter stick
>
> 3-L clear plastic bottle or 1-gal glass bottle
>
> black paper
>
> soil
>
> water

You may have noticed at night that as you move away from bright lights, the brightness decreases until they are no longer visible (i.e., intensity decreases rapidly as the distance from the light source increases.) The opposite also holds true, as you move toward a light, the closer you get, the brightness increases. You are going to determine if there is a mathematical relationship between light intensity and distance.

Procedure

1. Mark off a distance of 1.5 m from the light source. Divide the distance into 10-cm intervals. Place the light source on the 0-cm mark. Place a shoebox, with a small hole in the end over the light source. The light source should be at the small hole. Tape the light source and box in position to keep it from moving during the experiment. Place the light sensor at the point 10 cm from the light source. Make sure that the light sensor is pointed directly at the light source. Make sure that nothing obstructs the path between the light source and the sensor when readings are taken. Remove brightly colored objects from near the light source. Individuals should stand behind the sensor when readings are taken because this could otherwise cause erroneous intensity readings.

2. Set up the CBL system.

3. Collect the data by positioning the end of the sensor at the point 10 cm from the light source. Turn on the light. Wait 5 seconds. Record the data pair of light intensity and distance. Move the light sensor to 20 cm. Wait 5 seconds and collect the data. Continue collecting data in 10-cm intervals until a distance 1.5 m.

4. Record the light intensity values in the Data Table for Part One. What do you think will happen to the light intensity as distance increases? Why?

Data Table for Part One

Distance (cm)	Light Intensity (mW/cm^2)
10	
20	
30	
40	
50	
60	
70	
80	
90	
100	
110	
120	
130	
140	
150	

Part Two: Effect of Water on Light Intensity

Procedure

1. Place the 3-L plastic bottle or 1-gal glass bottle on a table and fill it with water. Wrap the black paper around the bottle, covering all the sides. Mark the paper on the outside of the bottle in 5-cm intervals. The bottom will be 0 cm. Place a shoebox with a small hole in the top of the box over the light source. The light source should be at the small hole. Tape the light source and box in position to keep it from moving during the experiment. The light source will be at 0 cm. Place the empty bottle on the top of the box over the light source. Mark off the distances of 5-cm intervals from the light source to the top of the bottle. Place the light

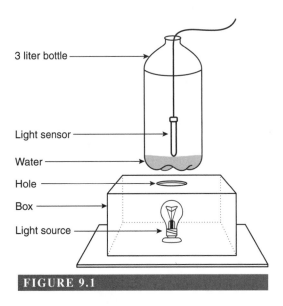

3 liter bottle

Light sensor

Water

Hole

Box

Light source

FIGURE 9.1

sensor through the opening of the bottle until it reaches a point at the bottom of the bottle next to the light source, as in Figure 9.1. Make sure that the light sensor is pointed directly at the light source. (If you do the experiment in a dark room, you do not need to use the shoebox.)

2. Set up the CBL.
3. Collect the data by positioning the end of the sensor at the point 0 cm from the light source (bottom of the empty bottle.) Turn on the light. Wait 5 seconds. Record the data pair of light intensity and distance. Turn off the light. Remove the light sensor from the bottle. Add water to the bottle to a depth of 5 cm. Lower the light sensor into the bottle to the surface of the water (5 cm) level. Turn on the light. Wait 5 seconds. Record the data pair of light intensity and distance. Turn off the light. Remove the light sensor. Add water to the 10 cm level. Lower the light sensor into the bottle to the surface of the water (10 cm) level. Turn on the light. Wait 5 seconds. Record the data. Continue collecting data in 5-cm intervals until the bottle is filled with water.
4. Record the light intensity values in the Data Table for Part Two.

Data Table for Part Two

Distance (cm)	Light Intensity (mW/cm^2)
.10	
5.0	
10.	
15	
20.	
25	
30.	

Part Three: Effect of Sediment Suspended in Water on Light Intensity

Repeat the experiment for Part Two by replacing the tap water with water to which sediments or soil has been added (muddy water). Start with the full bottle of muddy water and be sure you shake it well and often. Record your observations in Data Table for Part Three. What do you think will happen to the light intensity level when sediment is added to the water?

Data Table for Part Three

Distance (cm)	Light Intensity (mW/cm^2)
0.0	
5.0	
10.	
15	
20.	
25	
30.	

REFLECTIONS AND EXTENSIONS

Part One

1. Graph your data. Plot the distance (cm) on the horizontal axis and light intensity on the vertical axis.

2. Describe your graph.

3. Calculate the power regression equation and discuss the fit.

4. A light intensity curve showing an inverse square relationship looks like Figure 9.2.

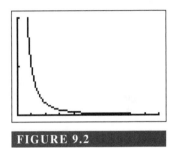

FIGURE 9.2

How well does your graph compare with this graph? Describe any differences.

5. If the light intensity and distance fit an inverse square relationship, doubling the distance would cause light intensity to be 1/4 as great. See how well your data fit by dividing the light intensity at 40. cm by the light intensity at 20. cm. Repeat this by dividing the light intensity at 80. cm by the light intensity at 40. cm. How close is your value to 1/4 (i.e., 0.25)?

6. Do your data support an inverse square relationship for light intensity and distance? Explain.

7. If you moved the light sensor 4 times further from the light, by what amount would the light intensity change?

8. According to scientific theory, the correct model for light intensity versus distance is an inverse square relationship. This relationship is expressed mathematically:

$$Y = \frac{A}{X^2}$$

Is this consistent with your data? Explain.

9. What will be the effect of a brighter bulb on the value of A? What is the effect on the value of Y?

10. Summarize the results of the experiment.

11. Test other light sources and compare the results.

12. The wavelength of red light is 750. nm, and that of violet light is 400. nm. Find the frequencies of these two extremes of visible light. All waves obey the equation $c = \lambda v$ where c represents the speed of light, 3.00×10^8, λ is the wavelength of the light, and v is its frequency. What is the frequency of red light in Hz? What is the frequency of violet light in Hz?

13. Visible light covers a frequency range of about 4.3×10^{14} Hz (red) to 7.5×10^{14} Hz (violet). What is the relationship between wavelength, or color, and frequency?

14. The energy carried by a photon is $E = hv$ where h is Planck's constant or $6.626. \times 10^{-34}$ J·s. What is the energy carried by a "red" photon? A "violet" photon?

15. Summarize the relationship between wavelength, frequency and energy.

Part Two

1. Determine the average light intensity for each distance.

2. Graph your data. Plot the distance (cm) on the horizontal axis and average light intensity on the vertical axis.

3. Does the light intensity–distance relationship in water have the same pattern as the light intensity–distance in Part One?

4. How well does your graph compare with the graph in Part One? Describe any differences.

5. Do your data for water support an inverse square relationship for light intensity and distance? Explain.

6. Water absorbs light so that even in clear water, not even 1% of the light that enters the ocean reaches a depth of 100 m. This effect is predicted with a relationship called the light extinction formula.

$$I_d = I_o e^{-kd}$$

This formula states that the intensity of light at the surface of the ocean (I_o) will decay at an exponential rate as depth (d) increases. The constant controlling this decay rate is the clarity of the water (k). Do your data support this relationship? Explain.

7. Rearrange the light extinction equation to calculate k. What is the value for k for your water?

Part Three

1. Graph your data. Plot the distance (cm) on the horizontal axis and average light intensity on the vertical axis.

2. How well does your graph compare with the graph in Part Two? Describe any differences.

3. What is the effect of adding sediments to the water on the light intensity?

4. What is the exponential regression equation for the data in the Data Table for Part Three? What is the rate of exponential decay?

5. Rearrange the light extinction equation to calculate k. What is the value for k for the sediment carrying water?

6. When the water is clear will the light extinction rate (k) be larger or smaller than in sediment carrying water?

7. If k is larger, will more or less light penetrate the water?

8. Summarize the relationship of the light extinction rate (k) to the amount of light that penetrates the water.

CHAPTER TEN

Subatomic Particles and Periodic Functions

PURPOSE

In this investigation, you will develop vocabulary specific to the structure of the atom, establish the background for obtaining numbers of subatomic particles given nuclear symbols for particular isotopes of an element, and investigate the existence of what is known as periodicity for the elemental properties of electronegativity and atomic radius.

FOUNDATIONS

History of the Atom

Recall that the ancient Greeks pondered the nature of matter as far back as 500 BC. During this time the ideas of *atomos* and *hyle* emerged. Also recall that *hyle* was Aristotle's idea that all matter came from only four elements: earth, air, fire, and water. Because of Aristotle's reputation, the idea of the existence of atoms remained submerged for many centuries.

The era between 400 BC and 1661 AD is sometimes called the dark ages of atomic theory. This time roughly corresponds to the Middle Ages and the emergence of the alchemist. The alchemist recognized three elements: sulfur, mercury, and salt (a compound, not an element). Also, alchemists were able to develop many experimental techniques that are still used today; for example, distillation, extraction, filtration, and chromatography. However, the idea of atoms as fundamental particles remained in obscurity.

In 1808 John Dalton proposed the first atomic theory. This theory was an induced theory because it lacked experimental support. Over the next century, though, many other scientists contributed to the unraveling of the secrets of the atom. It is now well established by experimental evidence that atoms exist, and they are composed of subatomic particles. Two major nuclear subatomic particles are the protons and neutrons. These particles are collectively called the nucleons, and they reside in the nucleus of the atom. The electrons exist outside the nucleus in what are called orbitals. Orbitals are areas of probability outside the nucleus where electrons are said to exist most frequently. Sometimes orbitals are referred to as electron clouds.

Historically, scientists like J. J. Thomson, William Thomson (aka Lord Kelvin), Wien, Planck, Einstein, Rutherford, Bohr, de Broglie, Schrödinger, Heisenberg, and Chadwick have made major contributions to the workings of the atom. J. J. Thomson (1897) is credited with naming and describing the electron (electrons were actually discovered by Crookes in 1886, but he didn't know what they were). William Thomson is credited with developing the classical Plum Pudding model of the atom. By characterizing the electron, he realized that electrons are part of the atom and that atoms also have a positive part that remains when the electrons are stripped away; hence, electrons are negatively charged. In his model he described the atom like a plum pudding: the volume of the atom was covered by positive sphere (pudding), and the raisins depicted the scattered electrons. In 1898 Wien discovered the proton and established it as part of an atom. In 1900 Planck introduced his quantum theory, which states that some kinds of energy are given off not continuously but in discrete units, which he called quanta. By 1908 Einstein had extended Planck's quantum theory to describe electrons in atoms. Einstein proposed that electrons in atoms occupy quantized energy levels.

Rutherford (1911) disproved Thomson's model of the atom and determined that the nucleus was centered within the atom. According to Rutherford, most of the mass of the atom was concentrated in a very small center and the electrons were seen to occupy the large volume around the nucleus that was mostly empty space; however, it wasn't known how the electrons were arranged in that space. This revolutionary theory was one of the results of his famous gold foil experiment. In his research, Rutherford took a very thin piece of gold foil (a layer of gold about .00004 cm, or 1000 atoms, thick) and shot the foil with alpha particles (helium nuclei). Expecting the large alpha particles to pass straight through the foil but discovering that they bounced off the foil at various angles, Rutherford had to reorganize his thinking into what is now referred to as the *nuclear atom.* Bohr (1913) decided that the electrons existed outside the nucleus in what he called orbits; orbits have certain energies and are certain specific distances from the nucleus. The Rutherford-Bohr model of the atom is also called the Planetary Model because it was once said that the electrons orbited the nucleus like the planets around the sun. Today, it is commonly thought that these orbits are better described in mathematical (quantum mechanical) terms. We think of what is now called an orbital as the most probable location of an electron traveling at a particular speed with a certain momentum. In 1924 de Broglie discovered that moving electrons behave like waves. This idea led to what is known as the wave–particle duality of nature. Heisenberg (1925) further described the positions of the electrons and developed what is called his Uncertainty Principle: it is not possible to know exactly where rapidly moving particles like electrons are at any given time. Schrödinger (1926) combined de Broglie's and Heisenberg's findings and gave rise to our modern concept of the atom, the Wave-Mechanical Model. Chadwick (1932) is usually credited with the discovery of the neutron more than 20 years after Rutherford had discovered the nucleus. (Chadwick was one of Rutherford's graduate students.)

Introduction to Subatomic Particles

The Bohr Model of the atom is still a good teaching tool for beginning to learn where the various parts of the atom are. In Figure 10.1, note the various areas of the atom and the subatomic particles present.

The nucleus contains most of the mass of the atom, and the remainder of the volume of the atom is composed of mostly empty space. The electron

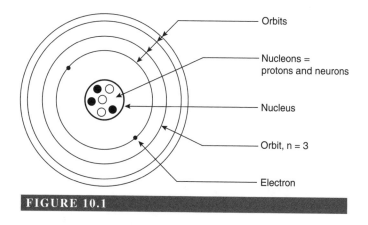

- Orbits
- Nucleons = protons and neurons
- Nucleus
- Orbit, n = 3
- Electron

FIGURE 10.1

(mass = 9.11×10^{-23} g) exists outside the nucleus. The electron consists of a very small mass and a negative charge. The proton in comparison to the electron has a substantially larger mass. The masses of the proton and neutron (also located in the nucleus) are similar. The nuclear particles of proton and neutron combine to give the approximate mass of the atom. The number of these so-called nucleons gives an atom its mass number. **Mass number** is the sum of the number of protons and neutrons. The number of protons is called the **atomic number.** In a neutral atom, the number of protons is the same as the number of electrons. The number of protons identifies the element. If you know the atomic number, then you know the element. If the number of protons changes, then the element is changed. Electrons can be lost or gained. A charged atom, called an **ion,** with an extra electron has an overall negative charge. A negatively charged ion is called an anion. When an atom loses an electron, it leaves the atom with an overall positive charge, and the particle is now called a cation. We can indicate all of this information in what is known as a nuclear symbol of the element. For example, in the following nuclear symbol on the left side, the superscript indicates the mass number, and the subscript indicates the atomic number for this particular calcium cation. It is called a cation because of the overall positive charge, 2^+. The charge of the atom is indicated by a superscript on the right side of the elemental symbol. This particular calcium cation has a mass number of 40 and the atomic number 20 with two less electrons than protons, or 18 electrons. The subscript on the right side of the elemental symbol is reserved for identifying the number of atoms needed in a chemical formula (e.g., Ca_3P_2).

$$_{20}^{40}Ca^{2+}$$

Sometimes this particular type of calcium is called calcium-40. There is also another type of calcium, called calcium-41. The nuclear symbol for this isotope of calcium has a greater mass number than the previous one:

$$_{20}^{41}Ca^{2+}$$

It has a greater mass number because it has an extra neutron in the nucleus. The number of protons has remained the same (20) and the element is still calcium, but the mass number (41) has increased due to an additional neutron in the nucleus of the atom. Isotopes are two different nuclides of the same element: same number of protons with differing number of neutrons. When you look at the periodic table, you will see that it is arranged by the order of increasing atomic numbers of the elements. The other number present (usually written underneath the element's symbol) is the averaged mass numbers or the atomic mass of all of that element known to exist. The average mass of calcium is 40.08 atomic mass units (amu). This average is calculated by taking into account the relative abundance of all the isotopes of calcium. Calcium-40 has a relative abundance of 92% and calcium-41 is present at 8%. [40(.92) + 41(.08) = 40.08 amu]

Introduction to Periodicity

It has been said that the periodic table of elements is the most predictive tool in science, but the periodic table has not always appeared as it does today. The development of the periodic table used today is mostly attributed to the contributions of a Russian scientist, Mendeleév (circa 1871). He based his arrangement of the then known elements in the order of their atomic masses, and then tried to put them in families that exhibited similar characteristics. This almost worked, but there were a few elements that when placed on the periodic table according to the atomic masses simply did not fall into the correct groups. However, from this novel invention, the first Periodic Law was established: elements are arranged on the periodic table according to their increasing atomic masses. The advantage of this display allowed Mendeleév to predict properties of yet to be discovered elements by averaging the characteristics of the elements above and below the missing element, and for the most part his predictions were proved correct when the missing elements were finally discovered.

Spotlight on the APP: Periodic

Some calculators have added an APP that allows one to simulate Mendeleév's experiments. From the APPS program select Periodic, then press the WINDOW key for various OPTIONS. From this selection you can highlight various regions of the periodic table (e.g., the metalloids), you can see an expanded version of the periodic table, highlight a particular block (e.g., *s, p, d,* or *f*), or you can study various periodic properties (e.g., electronegativity, atomic radius). Periodic properties can be graphed, or you can simply obtain specific data for most elements.

Unfortunately, Mendeleév's arrangement of the elements had a major flaw. In the late 1800s secrets of the atom in the form of the existence of some subatomic particles (electrons and protons) had been discovered. By the early 1900s a young scientist was able to correct Mendeleév's mistake and establish a second Periodic Law: elements are arranged on the periodic table according to their increasing atomic number (i.e., the number of protons). This arrangement allowed Mosely (circa 1914) to place the elements in sequential order and in the correct families according to their reactivity.

Four of the many properties of elements exhibit what is known as periodicity. These characteristics are electronegativity, ionization energy, electron affinity, and atomic radius. Electronegativity is the ability of an atom to attract an electron pair to itself. Ionization energy is the amount of energy needed to remove an electron from an atom (first ionization energy) and subsequent electrons from the appropriate ions (second, third, fourth, etc. ionization energies). Electron affinity is the ability of an atom to accept an electron, and atomic radius is defined as half the distance between the nuclei of two touching atoms. In this investigation we will study the periodic properties of electronegativity and atomic radius.

Exercise. Mendeleév arranged the elements known at that time on what is now called a periodic table. Actually, this first periodic table was simply a collection of elemental data written on his office's blackboard. Pretend that you are Mendeleév and that you knew that your table of elements was missing one element under silicon, Si. Using the properties that you can obtain from your graphing calculator (or other source), predict the unknown element's properties. He called this missing element eka-silicon, or the element under silicon. Complete the following table.

Atomic Symbol	Atomic Number	Atomic Weight	Atomic Radius (pm)	Density (g/cm^3)	Electronegativity
C	6				
Si	14				
eka-silicon	XXX	XXX	XXX	XXX	XXX
Sn	50				

Obtain the missing data for C, Si, and Sn. We will use the linear regression function on the graphing calculator to predict the values for eka-silicon. First exit the PERIODIC program using 2nd QUIT. Next press the APPS key and go to SciTools. Press ENTER and select DATA/GRAPHS WIZARD (3). Select DATA by pressing Y=. In L1 enter the given atomic numbers, in L2 enter the atomic weights, in L3 enter the atomic radii, in L4 enter the densities, and in L5 the electronegativities. Now use 2nd QUIT to return to the DATA/GRAPHS WIZARD screen. Select PLOT DATA with the WINDOW key. Select SCATTERPLOT with the Y= key. Let L1 be the independent variable and L2 be the dependent variable. By pressing 2nd QUIT, you bring up the CHOOSE A FIT menu. After pressing the ENTER key, press TRACE to view the graph of the linear regression line. Pressing the up arrow once will allow you to trace the data that have been entered for Y1 (atomic weight). The atomic number for eka-silicon is 32. Enter the number 32 followed by ENTER to get the predicted atomic weight of this element. Press 2nd QUIT to return to the DATA/GRAPHS WIZARD and repeat the steps to predict the remaining values for eka-silicon. This unknown element is now known to be germanium, Ge. Return to the Periodic Table APP to obtain the actual values for germanium. Compare the predicted values to the actual.

Mathematics Foundation

Periodicity is an important concept in mathematics as well as in science. Many students begin studying patterns in elementary school and expand the pattern ideas throughout their study of mathematics in middle school and high school. The classic use of periodic functions is in trigonometry when the trigonometric functions are defined and graphed. The first use of trigonometry, which was developed by the Greeks, was to measure sides and angles of triangles in areas such as architecture, navigation, surveying, and astronomy. After calculus was developed in the seventeenth century, trigonometric relationships were thought of as functions with periodic properties. The applications of trigonometric functions can be seen in sound and light wave theory, pendulums, planetary orbits, and periodic trends as related to the increasing atomic number of the elements.

The definitions of the six trigonometric functions using the lengths of the sides of a right triangle follow:

$$\text{sine (sin) } \theta = \frac{\text{Opposite side}}{\text{Hypotenuse}} \qquad \text{cosecant (csc) } \theta = \frac{\text{Hypotenuse}}{\text{Opposite side}}$$

$$\text{cosine (cos) } \theta = \frac{\text{Adjacent side}}{\text{Hypotenuse}} \qquad \text{secant (sec) } \theta = \frac{\text{Hypotenuse}}{\text{Adjacent side}}$$

$$\text{tangent (tan) } \theta = \frac{\text{Opposite side}}{\text{Adjacent side}} \qquad \text{cotangent (cot) } \theta = \frac{\text{Adjacent side}}{\text{Opposite side}}$$

Remembering *sohcahtoa* may help you learn the basic trigonometric functions: *soh* ⇒ sine is opposite over hypotenuse; *cah* ⇒ cosine is adjacent over hypotenuse; *toa* ⇒ tangent is opposite over adjacent.

Now we look at the graphs of these functions using a graphing calculator to discuss periodic functions. The concepts of amplitude, period, vertical displacement, and horizontal displacement will be discussed.

Amplitude is the absolute value of one-half the vertical distance between the highest and lowest points of the graph (or the distance from the baseline or horizontal axis to the top of a peak of a wave). It is measured in units of the *y*-axis. Amplitude can be thought of as a dilation. A dilation is a graph expanding or contracting.

Period is how often a graph repeats itself. It is measured in units of the *x*-axis. Period can also be thought of as a dilation. If the *x*-axis is defined by time, then the number of peaks per unit of time is known as the frequency of the wave function.

Vertical displacement is the distance a graph is moved up or down. It can be thought of as a translation. A translation is a graph being picked-up and moved without changing its shape or size.

Horizontal displacement is the distance a graph is moved left or right and can be thought of as a translation.

When using these concepts with trigonometric functions, you can use the general trigonometric function below with sine or cosine.

$$f(x) = C + A \cos(Bx - D)$$

Using the above equation:

> Amplitude $= |A|$
>
> Period $= 360°/B$
>
> Vertical displacement $= C$ units up if $C > 0$ or C units down if $C < 0$.
>
> Horizontal displacement $= D$ in the opposite direction of the sign of D in the given equation. This happens because the sign of D in the general equation is negative.

Example. Identify the amplitude, period, vertical and horizontal displacements (shifts) for the following equation; then graph the equation using your calculator. Be sure your calculator is in degree mode.

$$f(x) = 3 - 2\cos(4x + 180°)$$

Looking at the graph we see Figure 10.2.

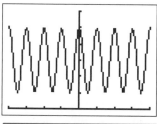

FIGURE 10.2

By tracing on the graph and/or using the formula, we can determine that the amplitude of the graph is 2, the period is 360/4, or 90 degrees, the vertical shift is 3, and the horizontal shift is to the left 180 degrees.

INVESTIGATION

Purpose. In this investigation you will investigate the existence of subatomic particles and what is known as periodicity, used to describe trends of elemental properties such as electronegativity and atomic radius. You will be given most of the data necessary, but you will be asked to predict missing values. Periodic functions are those in which the general trends repeat every period. There are 7 horizontal rows, or periods, on the periodic table that run across the table from left to right. The columns on the periodic table are called families or groups.

Materials

> subatomic particles worksheet
>
> subatomic particles answer sheet
>
> graph paper (scaled and regular)
>
> graphing calculator

Part One: Subatomic Particles

Procedure.   Complete the worksheet.

Subatomic Particles Worksheet

Fill in the blanks using the correct vocabulary from this chapter. Place your answers on the answer sheet that follows.

The nucleus of an atom consists of (1) and (2). The (3) of an atom gives the number of protons, and consequently identifies the element. The (4) of an atom gives the number as nucleons (5) and (6), which are subatomic particles found in the nucleus.

The symbols for the elements are often written with (7) at the lower left and (8) at the upper left (e.g., the symbol $_{19}^{40}K$, which represents the uncharged potassium isotope with 19 (9), 19 (10), and 40 (11) (19 (12) plus 21 (13)). When atoms are referred to as *charged,* their number of (14) can be more or less than their number of (15), which only changes when the atom changes. A positive ion is called a (16) and a negative ion is called a (17). A potassium ion, K^+, has 19 (18) and 18 (19). The fact that only 18 (20) are present indicates that the potassium ion has lost one (21). An oxygen ion has (22) protons and (23) electrons, indicating that the ion has gained two (24).

Atoms of the same element may differ in the number of (25) in the nuclei. When atoms have the same (26) but different number of (27), they are called (28) of that element. There are two naturally occurring (29) of chlorine. Because they are different forms of the same element, both (30) have the same (31), 17. One has a (32) of 36, and the other has a (33) of 38. The average (34) of chlorine is 35.457 amu, which falls between the (35) of 36 and 38 for chlorine.

Name	Nuclear Symbol	Atomic Number	Number of Protons	Number of Neutrons	Mass Number	Number of Electrons	Charge
(36)	$_1^1H+$	(37)	(38)	(39)	(40)	(41)	(42)
(43)	(44)	1	(45)	(46)	3	(47)	0
(48)	(49)	11	(50)	12	(51)	(52)	0
(53)	(54)	(55)	13	13	(56)	(57)	+3
(58)	(59)	(60)	79	(61)	199	(62)	0
(63)	(64)	(65)	(66)	18	(67)	18	–2
carbon	$_6^{14}C$	6	(68)	8	(69)	6	(70)

Answer Sheet
Subatomic Particles Worksheet

1. _____   36. _____
2. _____   37. _____
3. _____   38. _____
4. _____   39. _____
5. _____   40. _____
6. _____   41. _____
7. _____   42. _____
8. _____   43. _____
9. _____   44. _____
10. _____   45. _____
11. _____   46. _____
12. _____   47. _____
13. _____   48. _____
14. _____   49. _____
15. _____   50. _____
16. _____   51. _____
17. _____   52. _____
18. _____   53. _____
19. _____   54. _____
20. _____   55. _____
21. _____   56. _____
22. _____   57. _____
23. _____   58. _____
24. _____   59. _____
25. _____   60. _____
26. _____   61. _____
27. _____   62. _____
28. _____   63. _____
29. _____   64. _____
30. _____   65. _____
31. _____   66. _____
32. _____   67. _____
33. _____   68. _____
34. _____   69. _____
35. _____   70. _____

Part Two: Periodicity

Procedure

1. Using the data in Table 10.1, plot the covalent radius of each element on the ordinate against its atomic number on the abscissa. (Make the abscissa on the longest side of the paper and choose the scale so that all the data will fit on one sheet.) Use scaled graph paper. This is Graph One.
2. Connect all adjacent points with a straight line.
3. When the graph is complete, find the tallest peaks. Label each of these peaks with the corresponding symbol of the element.
4. Note that both Tables 10.1 and 10.2 contain "?". For each "?" predict the missing value.

Graph One

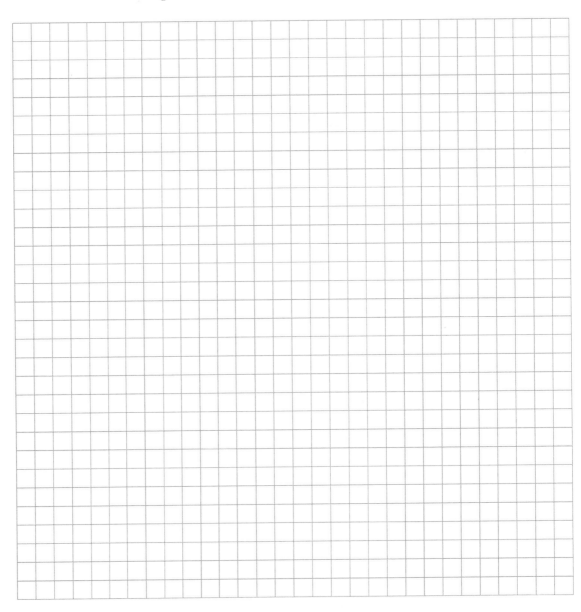

TABLE 10.1 Covalent Radii of Elements (Å [10^{-10} m])

ELEMENT	ATOMIC NUMBER	COVALENT RADIUS	ELEMENT	ATOMIC NUMBER	COVALENT RADIUS
H	1	.32	K	19	2.03
He	2	.93	Ca	20	1.74
Li	3	1.23	Sc	21	1.44
Be	4	.90	Ti	22	?
B	5	.82	V	23	1.22
C	6	.77	Cr	24	1.18
N	7	?	Mn	25	1.17
O	8	.73	Fe	26	1.17
F	9	.72	Co	27	1.16
Ne	10	.71	Ni	28	1.15
Na	11	1.54	Cu	29	1.17
Mg	12	1.36	Zn	30	1.25
Al	13	1.18	Ga	31	1.26
Si	14	1.11	Ge	32	1.22
P	15	1.06	As	33	1.20
S	16	1.02	Se	34	1.16
Cl	17	.99	Br	35	1.14
Ar	18	.98	Kr	36	1.09

TABLE 10.2 Electronegativity of Elements

ELEMENT	ATOMIC NUMBER	ELECTRONEGATIVITY (PAULING SCALE)	ELEMENT	ATOMIC NUMBER	ELECTRONEGATIVITY (PAULING SCALE)
H	1	2.1	K	19	.82
He	2	—	Ca	20	1.00
Li	3	.98	Sc	21	1.36
Be	4	1.57	Ti	22	1.54
B	5	2.04	V	23	1.63
C	6	2.55	Cr	24	1.66
N	7	3.04	Mn	25	1.55
O	8	3.44	Fe	26	1.83
F	9	3.98	Co	27	1.88
Ne	10	—	Ni	28	1.91
Na	11	.93	Cu	29	1.90
Mg	12	1.31	Zn	30	1.65
Al	13	?	Ga	31	1.81
Si	14	1.90	Ge	32	?
P	15	2.19	As	33	2.18
S	16	2.58	Se	34	2.55
Cl	17	3.16	Br	35	2.96
Ar	18	—	Kr	36	—

5. Repeat this process for the data found in Table 10.2 for electronegativity versus atomic number. (*Note:* The Pauling Scale is a relative scale, therefore there are no units associated with the property, and since the noble gases do not typically form bonds, no values are reportable. To indicate the missing data, connect the points on either side of the noble gases with a dashed line.) This is Graph Two.

6. Plot the same data on your graphing calculators. Adjust your scales and windows accordingly. Compare your hand-drawn graph to the one displayed by the calculator.

Graph Two

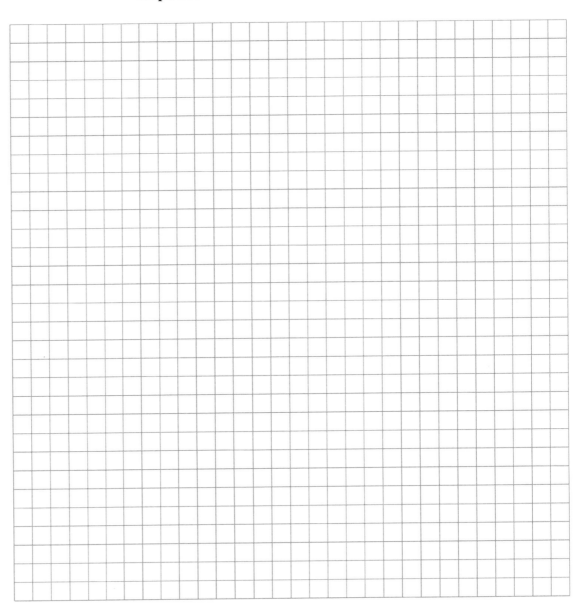

REFLECTIONS AND EXTENSIONS

1. What elements occupy the highest peaks on Graph One? Graph Two?

2. Look at a periodic table, do the elements on each graph have anything in common?

3. Divide both of your hand-drawn graphs into periods by drawing a dashed line the length of the ordinate after the elements He, Ne, and Ar. Describe the similarities of periods 2 and 3.

4. Using Graph One, determine the following:
   a. Period of each band

   b. Amplitude of each band

   c. Vertical shifts between the bands

5. Using your graphing calculator, pick two separate parts for Bands 2 and 3 (ending Band 3 at Ni) and fit each part of the four graphs using the regression features of the calculator. Write the equations for each of the four parts; then discuss similarities and differences.

6. In Table 10.1 missing data occur for the elements nitrogen and titanium. Predict values for the covalent radii (show work). Write these values on your graph.

7. In Table 10.2 missing data occur for elements aluminum and germanium. Predict values for these electronegativities (show work). Write these values on your graph.

CHAPTER ELEVEN

Aqueous Solutions and pH

PURPOSE

In this investigation you will determine the quantitative relationship between the concentration of hydrogen ions in solution and the pH value. The mathematical concepts utilized in this activity are the use of a logarithmic scale, graphing, and regression.

FOUNDATIONS

Exponential Notation

The equation $b^x = a$ is an exponential expression where b is the base and x is the exponent.

Example.   In the expression, $3^2 = 9$, 3 is the base, 2 is the exponent, and 9 is the answer.

Application Problem.   A new car depreciates 20% each year. Complete the following table. The value $V(t)$ of the car is in dollars and its age, t, is in years. Give each value to the nearest hundred. Complete the table; then use the values in your table to make a graph to show the relationship between $V(t)$ and t.

t	0	1	2	3	4	5
$V(t)$	14,400					

1. Graph the data calculated above, as shown in Figure 11.1.

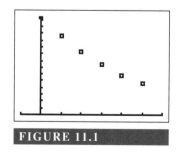

FIGURE 11.1

2. Use the following formula to write an equation of the graph.

$$V(t) = V_0(1 + r)^t$$

V_0 represents the initial amount, so in this problem $V_0 = 14{,}400$.

r represents the rate of growth or decay. Because the car is depreciating at 20%, r is $-.20$.

There is no need to replace t in this equation because it is the variable in which the function is defined.

So for this problem, the equation is $V(t) = 14{,}400(1 - .20)^t = 14{,}400(.8)^t$.

3. Use the exponential regression feature on your calculator to determine the equation. Check the graph by using your calculator.

Remember that to do any type of regression, data must be entered into L1 and L2. By using the information from the table, your L1 and L2 should look like Figure 11.2. Calculating exponential regression gives the results in Figure 11.3.

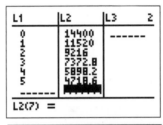
FIGURE 11.2

FIGURE 11.3

Logarithms

Definition: There are two logarithm keys on your calculator. One is the "log" key, which stands for the common logarithm with a base of ten. This logarithm is derived by starting with the exponential expression $10^x = a$. The expression can be rewritten in logarithmic form as $\log_{10} a = x$. It is important to be able to relate exponential and logarithmic expressions because often one form or the other is given, yet you need the other form. The reason it is possible to switch from one form to the other is that exponential and logarithmic functions are inverses of each other.

Examples

1. $10^3 = 1000$, so $\log 1000 = 3$
2. $10^{0.8} = 6.3$, then $\log 6.3 = .8$, which are approximations.

    Verify 1 and 2 using your calculator (Figure 11.4).

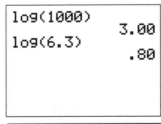
FIGURE 11.4

3. Since the logarithm of a number x is equal to the exponent to which 10 must be raised to give that number, we can say that log 10^2 equals 2, and log 10^{-5} equals -5.

Science Foundation

There are many products that are acidic or basic in nature. Some of these are naturally occurring and others are made commercially. A few examples of commercial products that are either acidic or basic are vinegar, fruit juices, carbonated beverages, baking soda, lye, household ammonia, and antacids. Several of these products include, as part of their labeling, their acidity content. Vinegar, fruit juices, carbonated beverages, and household ammonia are all considered to be solutions. Most solutions, but not all, are made of solids dissolved in water. A solution is a homogeneous mixture. Air is an example of a solution of gases; brass is an example of a solution of metals. Household ammonia (ammonium hydroxide [NH_4OH]) is made of ammonia gas (NH_3) dissolved in water. Solutions made from a solute (the substance that is dissolved) and the solvent (the dissolving medium) water are said to be aqueous solutions.

The ancient definition of an acid was something that tasted sour, and a base was a substance with a bitter taste. When litmus paper was developed, it allowed one to determine the acidity or basicity of a solution by the color the paper turned when it was wetted with the solution. Blue litmus paper turned red in the presence of an acid, and red litmus paper turned blue when wetted with a basic solution.

Another way to describe acidity is to calculate the concentration of the hydrogen ions present in solution. Historically, Arrhenius suggested that an acid was a substance that produced significant concentrations of the hydronium ion, H_3O^+, in water solutions, and bases were substances that produced hydroxide ions in water solutions. Brønsted and Lowry broadened this definition to include the idea that any substance that gave up protons was considered to be an acid, and if it accepted a proton it was considered to be a base. The broadest definition of acids and bases (as defined by Lewis) involves the actions of the outer orbital electrons. An acid is considered to be an electron pair acceptor and a base, an electron pair donor.

The determination of pH is a method used to quantify the concentration of acid present in solution. The formula for pH is as follows:

$$pH = -\log [H_3O^+]$$

Sometimes, instead of H_3O^+, we use only the simplified form H^+, which has the H_2O removed. In solution when a substance donates an H^+, the H^+ then combines with H_2O to form H_3O^+. Strong acids easily donate their H^+ in water, forming an aqueous solution. In chemical terms, their ionization reaction in water is said to go to completion. However, most acids are not strong, and consequently they only partially ionize in aqueous solutions. The same is true for weak and strong bases. Strong bases completely dissociate in aqueous solutions and weak bases do so only to a minimal extent. The related quantity to the concentration of acid in solution is called pH, and the related quantity to the concentration of base in solution is called pOH.

Example.   Determine the pH of an acid whose hydrogen ion concentration is equal to 2.5×10^{-5} M (the symbol M is used to denote molarity, or the concentration of a solution in moles of solute/liter of solution, mol/L).

$$pH = -\log [H_3O^+]$$
$$= -\log (.000025)$$
$$= 4.60$$

Example.   Determine the pOH of an acid whose hydrogen ion concentration is equal to 2.5×10^{-5} M. You can use one of the two methods below. The first method requires the use of the following formula:

$$pH + pOH = 14$$

so $4.60 + pOH = 14$; thus, $pOH = 9.40$.

The second method for determining the pOH requires you to first determine the concentration of the hydroxide ion, $[OH^-]$ and then use the formula for pOH:

$$pOH = -\log [OH^-]$$

To determine the $[OH^-]$ given the $[H_3O^+]$, you must use the relationship that states:

$$[H_3O^+] [OH^-] = 10^{-14}$$

In the previous example problem, the $[H_3O^+]$ is given as equal to 2.5×10^{-5} M, and so the $[OH^-]$ is calculated to be 4.0×10^{-10} M.

$$[H_3O^+] [OH^-] = 1 \times 10^{-14}$$
$$[OH^-] = \frac{1 \times 10^{-14}}{[H_3O^+]}$$
$$= 4.0 \times 10^{-10} \text{ M}$$
$$pOH = -\log [OH^-]$$
$$= -\log [4.0 \times 10^{-10}]$$
$$= 9.40$$

Using the pOH formula, the pOH is determined to be 9.40 when you take the opposite (i.e., negative) of the log of 4.0×10^{-10}. The rules for use of significant digits when dealing with concentration and pH or pOH are a little different than what we have previously discussed. The number of significant digits in the concentration will determine the number of significant digits that follow the decimal point in the pH or pOH.

pH Scale

The pH scale is a logarithmic scale. Solutions having a pH of 7 are said to be neutral (i.e., contain equal concentrations of H_3O^+ and OH^-, hydronium and hydroxide ions, respectively). If the $[H_3O^+]$ is greater than the $[OH^-]$, then the pH is less than 7, and the solution is acidic. If the $[OH^-]$ exceeds the $[H_3O^+]$, then the pH is greater than 7, and the solution is basic. A pH of 2 is not twice as concentrated as a pH = 1. A solution whose pH = 1 has a concentration of 10^{-1} M = 0.1 M; a solution whose pH = 2 has a concentration of 10^{-2} M = 0.01 M. Therefore, a pH of 2 is a factor of 10 times less acidic than a pH of 1.

Following is an example of a pH scale.

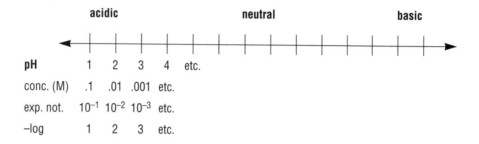

There is also a seldom-used pOH scale to denote the relative basicity of a base, $[OH^-]$, in solution. A solution with pOH of 1 has 10 times more OH^- ions than a solution with a pOH = 2.

INVESTIGATION

Part One: Determining pH of Household Products

Materials

> litmus paper strips
> red cabbage leaves
> 10-mL graduated cylinder
> 250-mL beaker
> 7 small beakers
> lemon-lime soda
> antacid tablets
> vinegar
> distilled water
> Drano
> baking soda
> ammonia

Procedure

1. Prepare a natural acid–base indicator by cutting up a few small leaves of red cabbage and boiling them in 50 mL of water until a purple solution is obtained.
2. Prepare solutions (about 10 mL) of the solids and obtain a small quantity (about 10 mL) of each of the following colorless aqueous solutions: (1) lemon-lime soda, (2) crushed antacid tablets in water, (3) vinegar,

(4) water, (5) dissolved Drano, (6) dissolved baking soda, and (7) household ammonia.

3. Determine the approximate pH of the above solutions by arranging them in order by color. (*Hint:* vinegar is an acid, water is neutral, and Drano is a base.) DO NOT THROW THE SOLUTIONS AWAY.

Solution	1	2	3	4	5	6	7
color							
pH							

Part Two: pH Curve

Materials

    vinegar

    distilled water

    100-mL graduated cylinder

    medium size beaker

    pH meter or pH probe

    eye dropper

    graphing calculator

Procedure

1. Put 50 mL of distilled water in a beaker. Record the pH in the following table. You may use a pH probe attached to a calculator or a pH meter.
2. Add 1 drop of vinegar to the water, take the pH and record it.
3. Continue adding 1 drop, taking pH and recording value for 25 drops; then complete the table.

Vinegar (drops)	0	1	2	3	4	5	6	7	8	9	10	11	12	13
pH														

Vinegar (drops)	14	15	16	17	18	19	20	21	22	23	24	25	30	35
pH														

Vinegar (drops)	40	45	50	60	70	80								
pH														

4. Graph the data from the table above on the graphing calculator. Sketch the graph below.

5. What type of equation does the graph represent?

6. Use the regression feature on the calculator to find the best-fit regression equation and write it here.

7. How does this equation relate to the scientific explanation of pH?

8. Measure the pH of pure vinegar. Does your solution ever reach this value? Why or why not?

9. Go back to the solutions you made in Part One and measure the pH of each using the pH meter. Record your answers then compare them to the estimates you got by using litmus paper.

Part Three: Testing Consumer Products

Background.   Vinegar is a solution of acetic acid, CH_3COOH, in water. Its molecular weight (or molar mass) is 60.0 g/mol. Vinegar, like many other products meant for human consumption, is strictly controlled by governmental agencies. In this investigation you will determine whether the stated acidity on the label of the vinegar bottle has been accurately reported. Acetic acid is a weak acid, which can be neutralized by adding a few drops of a strong base. If a measured volume of vinegar is titrated with a standardized solution of NaOH (sodium hydroxide), a strong base, to its neutralization point (end point), we can determine the concentration of the acid in the vinegar. By titration we can find the number of moles of acetic acid in the vinegar sample, and using the molecular mass of acetic acid as 60.0 g/mol we can calculate the number of grams of acetic acid in the sample.

Number of moles CH_3COOH
= Number of moles OH^- (at the end point)
= Volume of NaOH $\times$ molarity NaOH (in vinegar)

The NaOH solution has been standardized for you. Look on the bottle for its molarity. Molarity is a unit of concentration equal to the number of moles of solute per liter of solvent. To determine the mass (number of grams) of acetic acid you have, multiply 60.0 g/mol by the number of moles.

The density of vinegar for all practical purposes is that of water: 1.0 g/mL. Therefore, if you know the number of mL of vinegar you started with, you can determine the mass of the vinegar sample.

$$\text{Mass \% acetic acid} = \frac{\text{Mass of acetic acid}}{\text{Mass of vinegar sample}} \times 100$$

Materials

1 Erlenmeyer flask
1 clean buret rinsed with NaOH
2–3 drops phenolphthalein
35 mL NaOH (standardized)
10 mL vinegar
graphing calculator

Procedure

1. Measure exactly 5.0 mL of vinegar into a clean Erlenmeyer flask. Add about 30 mL of distilled water and two or three drops of phenolphthalein solution. Phenolphthalein is an organic compound, which in this case will act as a chemical indicator signaling the point in the titration at which equal amounts of acid and base are present. In acidic solutions phenolphthalein is colorless; it is pink in the presence of excess base.
2. Fill a clean buret with the standardized NaOH solution. Titrate the vinegar solution with the standardized base. As you approach the end point, add the NaOH very slowly and stop the titration when the solution takes on a pink color that persists for at least 30 s. Record the volume of base used.
3. Repeat the titration with a second 5.0 mL sample of vinegar.

Data Table for Part Three

	TRIAL 1	TRIAL 2
volume of vinegar	_____ mL	_____ mL
M of NaOH (on the label!)	_____	_____
volume of NaOH (initial)	_____ mL	_____ mL
volume of NaOH (final)	_____ mL	_____ mL
volume of NaOH used	_____ mL	_____ mL

REFLECTIONS AND EXTENSIONS

1. Calculate the average for the volume used of NaOH.

2. Calculate the number of moles of NaOH used to neutralize the sample.

3. How many moles of acetic acid were there in the vinegar sample?

4. How much does a mole of acetic acid weigh?

5. How many grams of acetic acid were there in the sample?

6. How much did the sample weigh? (Density of vinegar is about 1.0 g/mL.)

7. What is the mass % acetic acid in the vinegar?

8. Calculate the percentage error of your average value and that reported on the label of the vinegar.

9. Given the concentration of hydrogen ions in a solution to be 3.89×10^{-2}, calculate the pH, pOH, and $[OH^-]$ for that solution. Is it acidic or basic?

10. If the pH of a solution is 11.34, determine the pOH, $[H^+]$, and $[OH^-]$.

CHAPTER TWELVE

Genetics and Population Statistics

PURPOSE

In this investigation, you will start with the basic science concepts of Mendelian genetics and their use in predicting genetic outcomes from mono-hybrid and dihybrid crosses, along with the concepts of population statistics. Also, in this investigation cytogenetics will be explored. Mathematical concepts utilized include ratios, percentages, an application of the distributive property, and probability.

FOUNDATIONS

Introduction to Mendelian Genetics

Gregor Mendel is credited with the discovery of how plants and animals inherit from their parents the traits they exhibit, and how they pass these traits on to their offspring. Mendel, an Austrian monk, studied the characteristics of garden peas, which led to the establishment of many of the initial laws of inheritance. Because of his keen observations and his ability to keep accurate records, Mendel was able to formulate and test several hypotheses based on his experimentation. What we know today as genetic factors, Mendel had never heard of. Yet because of the variety of pea that he selected, he was able to control many genetic patterns.

A **gene** is a unit of heredity. It is actually a sequence of chemical bases in the DNA molecule that "tells" the organism to do something. It carries information that causes the organism to produce some enzyme, for example, or to produce some structural protein at particular stages in its development. Mendel interpreted his data in the following way: There are two units of heredity—two "Elementes," as he called them—for each trait. When each parent plant (the P_1 generation) produces sex cells or gametes, it passes on only one of its two hereditary units. In the first cross between the tall and the short plants, the tall plant could pass on for this trait only a big T, and the short pea plant could pass on only a small t. Therefore, plants of the next generation, which is labeled as F_1 (for first filial) all have the units big T and little t. Mendel concluded that the hereditary unit for tall must have covered up or dominated the hereditary unit for short so that the first-generation cross between the tall pea plant and the short pea plant always produced tall pea plants (see the Punnett squares following). Because of his keen observational skills and meticulous experimental techniques, Mendel formulated the law of segregation and the law of independent assortment, which still hold true today.

P_1 Generation Cross

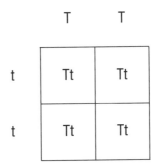

Introduction to Cytogenetics

Cytogenetics is the science of chromosome structure, function, and activity in meiosis and mitosis. Four nitrogenous bases, guanine (G), cytosine (C), adenine (A), and thymine (T), code all the genetic information found in DNA (deoxyribonucleic acid). Watson, Crick, and Franklin's experimental work led to the discovery of the double helical structure of DNA. However, only Watson and Crick received the Nobel Prize in 1953 because of the untimely death of Roslind Franklin. In eukaryotic cells, those with a *true* nucleus, chromatin (DNA) is found in the nucleus. Under a light microscope, the nucleus appears grainy and reticular in normal cells. (In cancerous cells the normally reticular chromatin appears clumped and the nucleus may be misshapen.) The major function of DNA is to provide the blueprint for the amino acid sequence of proteins. Genes are a specific segment of DNA. Ribonucleic acid (RNA) is made from DNA by a process known as transcription. The RNA, in turn, codes for the amino acid, making sure that they are in the proper sequence. The joining of the amino acids in the proper sequence to make a protein is called translation.

A rapidly dividing cell population undergoing metaphase is the best situation for making chromosome squashes. Cytogeneticists study chromosomes available from these spreads. Usually, the first evaluation made is to determine the number of chromosomes present. There are 46 chromosomes in the normal human cell: 22 pairs of homologous autosomes and two sex chromosomes. Next they will look at the chromosomes' size, arm ratio, centromere location, and bands in order to align them onto what is known as a karyotype. The purpose of karyotyping is to attempt to detect any structural abnormality present on a particular chromosome.

The karyotype table orders the chromosomes from the largest (pair 1) to the smallest (pair 22). This process allows for identification of the sex of the individual and any structural anomalies present. In the male, the sex chromosomes are an X and a Y; in the female, two X chromosomes are present. The two-chromosome situation is necessary because zygotes (fertilized eggs) are made from half-maternal and half-paternal chromosomes. Each parent contributes 23 chromosomes (a haploid set) from either a sperm or an ovum to the potential offspring, which consequently contains 46 chromosomes (diploid number) in their somatic cells. For humans, the count of 46 is the euploid species number. The sex of the offspring is determined by the father's sperm cell. In every human mating, there is a 50:50 chance of the child's being a boy or girl.

The female's XX chromosomes are positioned between chromosome pairs 7 and 8 on the karyotype, and the male's X is located in the same position, with his Y being placed after autosomal pair 22. (Sometimes you will see karyotypes with all the sex chromosomes listed last.) Chromosomal identification of a person is possible by looking at buccal smears of somatic cells under a light microscope. Buccal smears are obtained by scraping the lining of the cheek (the buccal cavity is the inside of your mouth). The somatic cells obtained from this procedure can then be spread on a slide and stained. In the female, one can see the presence of Barr bodies along the nuclear membranes of non-clumped cells. The Barr body is the inactive X chromosome of the female. Since males only have one X chromosome, they do not exhibit Barr bodies in their somatic cells.

The incidence of major chromosome aberration is 1 in 200, almost equally divided between autosomes and sex chromosomes. The most easily detected and common chromosome aberrations occur when cells containing too many or too few chromosomes are evaluated. Trisomy 21 (also called Down syndrome and mongolism), Klinefelter syndrome, and Turner syndrome are possible diagnoses that result from having too many or too few chromosomes. In Down syndrome the affected individual generally has three 21st chromosomes. These individuals have an extra chromosome in all the cells in their bodies. ("Mosaics" may have less than 100% of the cells affected and may not be as severely afflicted.) Children with Down syndrome are mentally retarded and usually have major phenotypic effects (e.g., low nasal bridge and protruding tongue along with Mongoloid slanted eyelids). Advancing maternal age at the time of conception increases the incidence of trisomy 21. In Klinefelter syndrome, the affected male has 47 chromosomes because of the XXY combination. Klinefelter syndrome occurs approximately once in every 500 male births. The Klinefelter male has small testes with decreased or absent spermatogenesis and will have a positive test for Barr bodies due to the presence of a second X chromosome. In Turner syndrome the affected female has only 45 chromosomes because of the lack of one of her X-chromosomes. The condition is usually denoted as 45,XO and has a rate of occurrence of about 1 out of 2500 female births. Females afflicted with Turner syndrome have primary amenorrhea. Other phenotypic characteristics include shortness of stature, webbing of the neck, and malformations of the head.

Figure 12.1 shows a karyotype of a normal male. Note the seven groups (A–G), and how chromosomes are arranged by decreasing size and centromere location. Band patterns are useful in the pairing of the chromosomes.

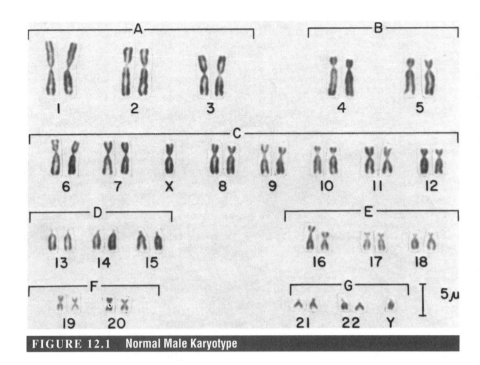

FIGURE 12.1   Normal Male Karyotype

Mathematics Foundation

Probability theory is used extensively in genetics. We will first review some basic definitions and probability rules; then we will use them in connection with genetics.

Experiment: an activity or occurrence with an observable result

Trial: each repetition of the experiment

Outcomes: possible results of each trial

Sample space: set of all possible outcomes. Written as S

Event: subset of outcomes of a sample space. Written as E

Probability of event *E*: P(*E*):

$$\frac{n(E)}{n(S)} = \frac{\text{Number in } E}{\text{Number in } S}$$

Complement of *E* is *E′*, and the sum of *E* and *E′* is 1, so $E = 1 - E'$, or $E' = 1 - E$.

Example.   Suppose a fair die is rolled.

1. What is the sample space?

   $S = \{1, 2, 3, 4, 5, 6\}$

2. What is the event of an even number?

   $E = \{2, 4, 6\}$

3. What is the probability of an even number being rolled?

   $P(E) = \dfrac{3}{6} = 0.5$

Example. Suppose a family has three children:

1. What is the sample space?

$S = \{ggg, ggb, gbg, bgg, bbg, bgb, gbb, bbb\}$

2. What is the event of two girls?

$E = \{ggb, gbg, bgg\}$

3. What is the probability of two girls?

$$P(E) = \frac{3}{8} = 0.375$$

4. What is the probability of at least one girl?

This can be done in two ways:

a. Using probability formula: $P(\text{At least one girl}) = \frac{7}{8}$

b. Using complement: $P(\text{At least one girl}) = 1 - P(\text{No girls}) =$
$1 - \frac{1}{8} = \frac{7}{8}$

The example demonstrates **theoretical probability.** Theoretical probability explains what is supposed to happen based on past experiences and the law of averages. Theoretical probabilities will always be the same. Experimental probability, which will be discussed in the next section, can change from one problem to the next.

Two events are **mutually exclusive** if they do not have any outcomes in common. That is, $P(A \cap B) = 0$. Two events are **independent** if the outcomes of one event do not affect the outcomes of the other event.

Conditional Probability: The probability of event B given event A has already occurred can be written as $P(B|A)$.

Addition Rule: Probability of event A or B:

$P(A \text{ or } B) = P(A) + P(B) - P(A \cap B)$, if not mutually exclusive

$P(A \text{ or } B) = P(A) + P(B)$, if mutually exclusive

Multiplication Rule: Probability of events A and B:

$P(A \text{ and } B) = P(A) * P(B)$, if independent

$P(A \text{ and } B) = P(A) * P(B|A)$, if not independent

Example. The following table represent a random sample of 1000 people, with M representing males, F representing females, C representing red–green colorblindness, and C' representing no colorblindness.

	M	F	TOTAL
C	42	7	49
C'	485	466	951
Total	527	473	1000

1. $P(M) = \dfrac{527}{1000} = .527$

2. $P(C) = \dfrac{49}{1000} = 0.049$

3. $P(M \mid C) = \dfrac{42}{49} = 0.857$

4. $P(F \mid C) = \dfrac{7}{49} = 0.143$ (or $1 - .857 = .143$)

5. $P(M \text{ or } C) = P(M) + P(C) - P(M \cap C)$

$= \dfrac{527}{1000} + \dfrac{49}{1000} - \dfrac{42}{1000} = \dfrac{534}{1000} = 0.534$

6. $P(M \text{ and } C) = P(M) \times P(C \mid M) = \dfrac{527}{1000} \times \dfrac{42}{527} = 0.042$

These values were calculated based on observations and data collected from 1000 people. This is an example of experimental probability. If we were to select another 1000 people and collect the data from them, we would most likely come up with a different set of answers.

Suppose you flip a coin 50 times and it comes up heads 20 times. For you, your experimental probability would be 20/50 or .4. But we know that the theoretical probability of coming up heads is .5. It is possible that you could get heads 50 times (possible, although highly unlikely) and have a probability of 1. You know that should not be right. If you repeat the coin flipping experiment enough times and collect a lot of data, your experimental probability should begin to be very close to the theoretical probability.

Let's revisit the experiment where you flipped the coin 50 times and came up with 20 heads. We decided that $P(\text{Heads}) = 20/50$. Another idea to discuss is that of **odds.** Odds, in this example, express a relationship between heads and tails. Based on $P(\text{Heads})$, we can find $P(\text{Tails})$ to be 30/50. Looking at the information of the number of heads and tails, we can say that the odds of getting a head would be 20:30, which could be reduced to a 2:3 ratio. Notice that while this gives the odds for heads, it also gives us information about the number of tails (30) as well as the total number of trials (50).

INVESTIGATION

Part One: Problem Solving

Before beginning these exercises, you might find it helpful to read through the definitions below. You may also need to refer to these definitions as you work through Part One.

Definitions

Allele: Alternate forms of the same gene, affecting a single characteristic and located at the same point or locus on homologous chromosomes.

Autosome: non–sex cell chromosome.

Dihybrid cross: A genetic cross involving a study of the inheritance of two different traits or characters. This type of cross considers how these two traits are inherited together.

Dominant: Describing a trait that appears whenever a gene for that trait is present. Its presence masks or hides the presence of a recessive trait.

Euploid: True number of chromosomes present. In humans, 23 pairs.

F_1: First filial generation: offspring of the P_1 parental cross.

F_2: Second filial generation: offspring resulting from the crossing of F_1 parents.

Gamete: Male or female sex cell (sperm or egg, respectively) containing half the number of chromosomes of the body cells.

Gene: Unit of heredity; a segment of locus of the chromosome that influences the expression of one trait.

Genetics: The science of heredity.

Genotype: The genetic makeup of an organism; the actual alleles of an organism, as contrasted to the phenotype, or visible characteristics, of an organism.

Heterozygous: Describing the condition in which members of a gene pair (alleles) determining a single trait are different on homologous chromosomes.

Homologous chromosomes: Two chromosomes, identical in size, shape, and centromere site, which carry genes controlling the same traits. One set of chromosomes is obtained from each parent.

Homozygous: Describing the condition in which members of a gene pair (the alleles) are identical on homologous chromosomes.

Monohybrid cross: A genetic cross involving the study of the inheritance of only one character or trait.

P_1: The parental generation with which a breeding experiment starts.

Phenotype: The visible characteristics of an organism, as contrasted to the genotype.

Punnett square: A diagram that reveals all possible genetic combinations and ratios of offspring from two parents provided that the gametes are properly identified and located on the diagram.

Recessive: Describing a trait that is masked or hidden in the presence of a dominant trait, but which is displayed in the absence of a dominant trait.

Segregation: The separation of genes into different gametes when chromosomes separate during meiosis.

Trait: A physical or chemical expression of inheritance.

Zygote: A fertilized egg.

Exercise 1. The following chart shows the results of Mendel's one-trait, or monohybrid, crosses using garden peas. Use your calculators to determine the ratios in each of the seven crosses that Mendel made. Formulate a hypothesis or generalization concerning the ratios he obtained. Is there some kind of pattern? Can you make a hypothesis that will include all these data?

P_1 CROSS	F_1 PLANTS	F_1 CROSS	F_2 PLANTS	ACTUAL RATIO
Seeds round $\times$ wrinkled	all round	round $\times$ round	5474 round 1850 wrinkled 7324 total	
Seeds yellow $\times$ green	all yellow	yellow $\times$ yellow	6022 yellow 2001 green 8023 total	
Flower Color red $\times$ white	all red	red $\times$ red	705 red 224 white 929 total	

Pods
inflated $\times$
  wrinkled
	all inflated	inflated $\times$
		  inflated
			882 inflated
			299 wrinkled
			1181 total	

Pods green $\times$ yellow	all green	green $\times$ green	428 green 152 yellow 580 total	
Flowers axial $\times$ terminal	all axial	axial $\times$ axial	651 axial 207 terminal 858 total	
Stems long $\times$ short	all long	long $\times$ long	787 long 277 short 1064 total	

Hypothesis or generalization:

Exercise 2. Some people can roll their tongues sideways; some people find it impossible to do this. Can you roll your tongue? Collect data from the people in your class. Report the actual and simplified ratios of those who can to those who cannot.

_____ (actual) _____ (simplified)

From the data collected, would you assume that tongue rolling is a dominant or recessive trait? _____

Provide information for the tongue-rolling trait, given the following situation in which T = tongue roller and t = non–tongue roller.

father = TT

mother = tt

1. What is the phenotype of the father? _____

2. What is the genotype of the father? _____

3. What is the phenotype of the mother? _____

4. What is the genotype of the mother? _____

5. What is the phenotype of the children? _____

6. What is the genotype of the children? _____

7. What percentage of the children are Tt? _____

Exercise 3. Complete the pedigree diagram in Figure 12.2 for the human genetic trait of tongue rolling. In this chart a square indicates a male and a circle indicates a female. A horizontal line connecting a square and a circle indicates a marriage, and the vertical lines down from the marriage indicate the children produced by that marriage. The shading of the square and circle symbols indicates which individuals have the dominant tongue-rolling trait. Using the genetic symbols and genotypes in your answers for Exercise 2 (1–6), write the genotypes and phenotypes below the squares and circles in the diagram.

Answer questions 1–7 below regarding this scenario.

The male child in the family previously described subsequently married with the results shown in Figure 12.3.

1. How many children are there? _____

2. What is the ratio of boys to girls? _____

3. If this couple had a fourth child, what are the odds of it being a boy? _____

4. What is the genotype of the wife? _____

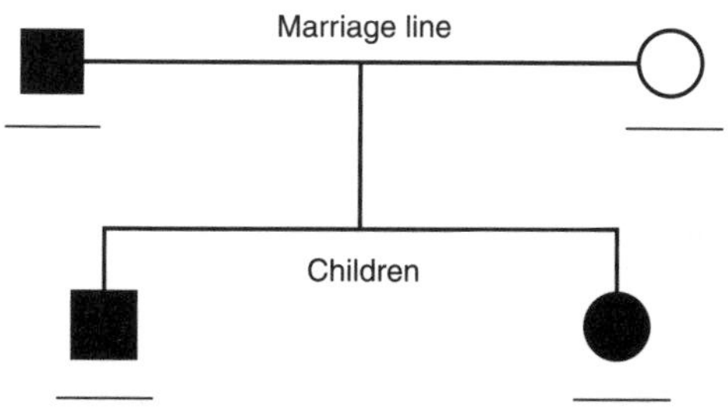

Marriage line

Children

FIGURE 12.2

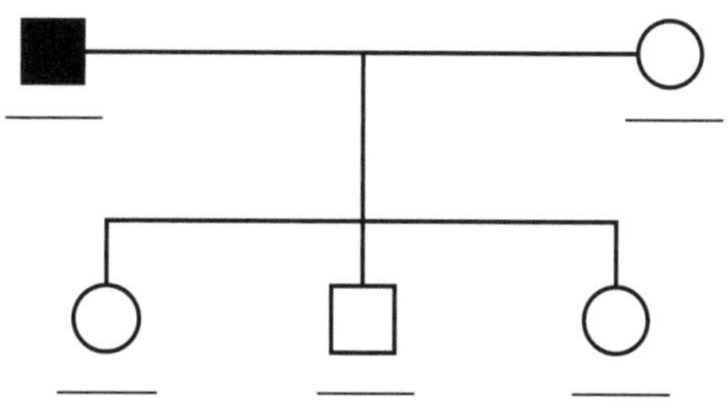

FIGURE 12.3

5. What are the genotypes of the children? _____

6. Who in the family can roll their tongue? _____

7. Why couldn't any of the offspring
   roll their tongues? _____

Exercise 4.   Because meiosis occurs when gametes are being formed, the gametes have only half the number of chromosomes that the body cells of an organism have. If you are given one or two or any number of pairs of genes located on different chromosomes, you should be able to indicate how they will be separated in the gametes.

From the following genotypes, determine the possible alleles in the gametes.

1. AA   _____ and _____

2. Aa   _____ and _____

3. AABB   _____ and _____

4. AaBB   _____ and _____

5. AABb   _____ and _____

6. Aabb   _____ and _____

7. aabb   _____ and _____

Exercise 5.   An easy way to determine the kinds of offspring that may result from a genetic cross of specific parents is to use a Punnett square, a device invented by an English geneticist of that name. In this square letters representing the alleles of males gametes are noted across the top and letters representing the alleles of female gametes are written down the left side, as in Figure 12.4.

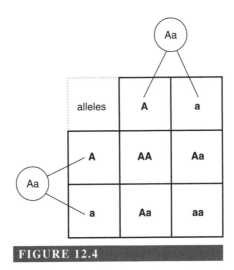

FIGURE 12.4

1. Suppose the male genotype is Bb and the female is Bb. Using these genotypes, complete the Punnett square. (It is customary to put the uppercase letter first, when it is combined with a lower case letter.)

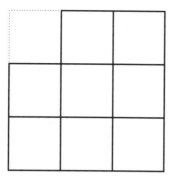

2. Suppose the female genotype is dd and the male is Dd. Using these genotypes, complete the Punnett square.

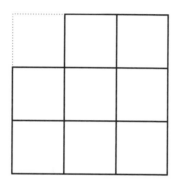

3. The following situations describe scenarios involving two traits. These types of Punnett squares are therefore sometimes called dihybrid crosses. Let B = black, b = white, R = rough, and r = smooth. In the P$_1$ generation, a black, smooth-coated guinea pig and a white, rough-coated guinea pig mated. The black, smooth-coated male is a homozygous BBrr, and the white, rough-coated female is a homozygous bbRR. They produced an F$_1$ generation of all black, rough-coated offspring. In the F$_2$ generation the offspring of the F$_1$ generation were interbred; specifically, a male heterozygous for both traits and a female homozygous dominant for color and heterozygous for coat condition.

P$_1$ Cross:

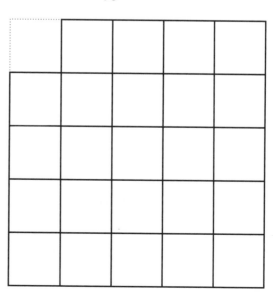

F$_1$ Cross

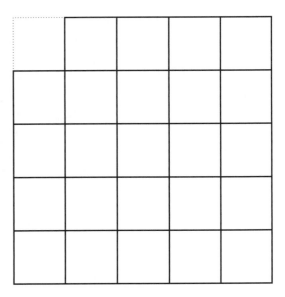

F$_2$ Cross

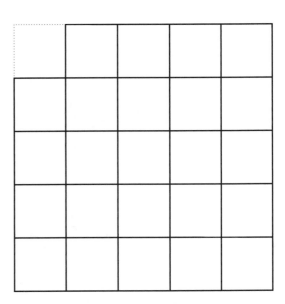

4. Give the F$_3$ genotypes and phenotypes with simplified ratios of occurrence.

Part Two: Cytogenetics Investigation

Materials

    slides, cover slips

    iodine solution (dilute) or other appropriate stain

    microscopes

    scissors

Exercise 1

1. Prepare a buccal smear by taking a toothpick and scraping the inside of your cheek.
2. Place the cells obtained on a glass slide.
3. Add one drop of iodine solution.
4. Place a cover slip on the top of the stained smear.
5. Look at the cells' nuclei around the nuclear membrane.
6. Count the number of cells that are flat with an observable nucleus.
7. Count the number of Barr bodies present in these cells.
8. Record the percentage of Barr bodies to cells present.

Data Table for Part Two, Exercise One

Number of Observable Cells	Number of Barr Bodies Seen	Percentage

Exercise 2.   Practice doing karyotyping by visiting www.biology.washington. edu/bsa/karyotype-shocked.html.

1. Cut out the chromosomes found on the squash in Figure 12.5.
2. Arrange them into a karyotype.
3. Identify the anomaly. _____

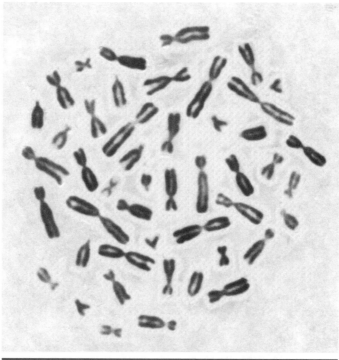

FIGURE 12.5   Chromosome Squash

Place your properly arranged karyotype here. (Do not glue it down until you are sure it is correct!)

— —   — —   — —   — —   — —
   1   2   3   4   5

— —   — —   — —   — —   — —   — —   — —
   6   7   8   9   10   11   12

— —   — —   — —   — —   — —   — —
  13   14   15   16   17   18

— —   — —   — —   — —   — —
  19   20   21   22   sex

REFLECTIONS AND EXTENSIONS

1. In cats the recessive gene for long hair is dominated by its allele for short hair. Suppose a heterozygous short-haired male cat is mated with a long-haired female. She has eight kittens, six with short hair and two with long hair. How do these numbers compare with the expected ratio?

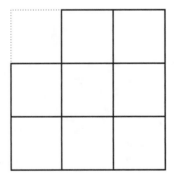

2. If you mated these two cats five more times and obtained a total of 42 offspring, why would you expect the actual number of long- and short-haired kittens to be closer to the predicted ratio?

3. What is the probability that an offspring in this mating has at least one dominant allele?

4. What is the probability that an offspring has at least one recessive allele?

5. What is the probability that an offspring has one recessive allele, given that the offspring has short hair?

6. DNA testing is used often in criminal investigations. Suppose you are studying three gene characteristics. Research has shown that 10% of the population have blue eyes, 5% have naturally blond hair, and 20% have fair skin.

    a. What is the probability that a randomly selected individual has all three characteristics, assuming the characteristics are independent?

    b. Do you think the assumption of independence is correct? Explain.

7. Some cattle have horns, and some are polled (without horns). The trait for polled is dominant. Black is dominant over red. What kinds and percentages of calves (i.e., give the genotypes and phenotypes with percentages of occurrence) would be expected from the mating of a heterozygous black, polled bull with a horned red cow?

CHAPTER THIRTEEN

Crystals and Geometry

PURPOSE

This investigation starts with the geometric study of Platonic solids, then connects these solids with the scientific study of crystals. Investigation Part Two (Growing Crystals) needs to be done early in the semester or school year because it takes about two months to grow a good crystal. The rest of the chapter should be done after the crystals have been grown. Growing crystals is both an art and a science. Whichever single large crystal you choose to grow, several laboratory sessions will be required. However, you do not have to spend a lot of time on this project, because the crystals will grow by themselves once you get them started. The mathematical concepts included are polygons, parts of the polygon, parallel lines, perpendicular lines, right angles, quadrilaterals, polyhedrons, Platonic solids, prisms, pyramids, and Euler's formula. The scientific concepts included are crystallography, systems of crystals, crystalline shapes found in nature, and x-ray diffraction.

FOUNDATIONS

Mathematics Foundation

Polygons are simple closed curves in two dimensions. This means that the polygon is made of line segments that do not cross themselves and form closed shapes. The line segments forming a polygon are called the **sides** of the polygon. The **vertex** (vertices is the plural form) is where two sides meet. Polygons are classified by number of sides or vertices.

A **regular polygon** has congruent sides (i.e., same shape and size) and congruent angles. **Parallel** sides never intersect. **Right angles** are formed when intersecting lines form 90° angles and these intersecting lines are said to be **perpendicular. Quadrilaterals** have special names that are defined by types of sides and angles.

QUADRILATERAL NAME	DESCRIPTION
Parallelogram	A quadrilateral with two pairs of opposite sides parallel.
Rhombus	A parallelogram with four equal sides.
Rectangle	A parallelogram with four right angles.
Square	A rectangle with four equal sides.
Trapezoid	A quadrilateral with at least one pair of parallel sides.

Polygon	Number of Sides or Vertices	Shapes
Triangle	3	△
Quadrilateral	4	▭
Pentagon	5	⬠
Hexagon	6	⬡
Heptagon	7	
Octagon	8	⯃
Nonagon	9	
Decagon	10	
Dodecahedron	12	
Icosahedron	20	
n-gon	n	

A **polyhedron** is a simple closed solid surface (exactly one interior with no holes, and hollow) made up of polygonal regions. They are three-dimensional, and the polygonal regions are called **faces.** The sides of each polygonal region are called **edges** of the polyhedron, and the vertices of the polygonal region are called **vertices** of the polyhedron. A **regular polyhedron** is a convex polyhedron (the segment connecting any two points in the interior of the polyhedron is itself in the interior) whose faces are congruent regular polygonal regions. The five regular polyhedrons are called Platonic solids after the Greek philosopher Plato, who studied them in the fourth century BC. He associated these solids to the four elements (earth–cube, air–octahedron, fire–tetrahedron, water–icosahedron) and the universe to the dodecahedron. Aristotle was a pupil of Plato. Recall from previous chapters that Aristotle believed that all matter was composed of one continual substance called *hyle* that was composed of these four elements connected by the natural sensations. (Refer to the diagram on the facing page.)

Three of the Platonic solids occur in nature in the form of **crystals** of sodium chloride (cube), sodium bromate (tetrahedron), and chrome alum (octahedron). The other two solids (icosahedron and dodecahedron) appear in skeletons of microscopic sea protozoa called radiolaria. These five regular polyhedrons are the only ones that have been found to exist in nature. The

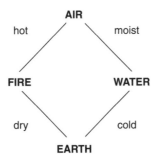

recently discovered (1980s) buckminsterfullerenes, or buckyballs, consist of a sphere of carbons that appears to look much like a soccer ball. The naturally occurring buckyball, isolated from carbon soot, contains 60 or more carbon vertices formed from interconnected five- and six-membered carbon rings. The highly symmetrical C_{60} is composed of 20 hexagons and 12 pentagons and has 32 faces. The discoverers of buckyballs received the Nobel Prize in chemistry in 1996. Two of the chemists are from Rice University, Professors Richard E. Smalley and Robert F. Curl, Jr., and the other prizewinner, Sir Harold W. Kroto, is from England.

REGULAR POLYHEDRA	DESCRIPTION
Cube	Composed of 6 congruent squares.
Tetrahedron	Composed of 4 equilateral triangles.
Octahedron	Composed of 8 equilateral triangles.
Icosahedron	Composed of 20 equilateral triangles.
Dodecahedron	Composed of 12 regular pentagons.

There are many other polyhedra such as prisms and pyramids. **Prisms** are composed of two congruent polygonal **bases** (opposite and congruent faces) in separate parallel planes connected by lateral faces that are parallelograms. **Pyramids** are formed by a single polygonal base and a point that is not in the plane of the base. Pyramids have triangular faces and are named by the polygon that forms the base such as a square pyramid, hexagonal pyramid, triangular pyramid, and so on.

Science Foundation

Crystallography is a mathematically exact science that classifies crystals with certain geometric shapes. Crystallography was first developed by Rene-Just Hauy in the late eighteenth and early nineteenth centuries. Christian Weiss developed the classification methods used today by dividing crystals into seven different crystal systems in the first part of the nineteenth century, and this system is in Table 13.1. A **crystal** is a solid piece of matter with definite geometric shape. The word *crystal* comes from the Greek roots meaning "clear ice." Crystals are bound by plane surfaces that are called **faces.** The shapes of crystals are determined by X-ray diffraction techniques. As the X-ray beam is bounced off the crystal, the angle of deflection is recorded.

TABLE 13.1 Systems of Crystals

TYPE	NUMBER OF FACES	SHAPE(S) OF FACES	PATTERN	REAL-WORLD EXAMPLES

Cubic	6	All squares	S
			S S S
			    S
			    S
				Silver, gold, diamond

Tetragonal	6	4 rectangles and 2 squares	S R1 S
			   R1
			   R1
			   R1
				zircon

Orthorhombic	6	3 pairs of rectangles with different sizes	R1
			    R2
			    R1
			R3 R2 R3
				topaz

Rhombohedral	6	6 rhombuses no right angles	RH1
			  RH1 RH1
			    RH1F
			RH1F RH1F
				calcite

Monoclinic	6	4 rectangles 2 parallelograms 16 right angles and 8 other angles	P1
			    R2
			    P1F
			R3 R2 R3
				gypsum

Triclinic	6	6 parallelograms no right angles	P1
			  P3 P2
			    P1F
			P2F P3F
				turquoise

Hexagonal	8	2 hexagons 6 rectangles	S S S
			   H
			S S S
			   H
				Ice, emerald, quartz

This allows for the determination of the size, shape, and bond angles of the crystal's vertices. These faces always intersect at angles that are characteristic of the substance in question. Crystals repeat themselves indefinitely in all directions. Snowflakes are very common crystals that result from the cooling of moist air.

Crystals have many applications. Crystals of such materials as diamond, ruby, and silicon also have industrial importance. Quartz crystals are used to generate electromagnetic radiation of a certain frequency. Solid state electronic devices are made from silicon or germanium crystals. Sodium chloride crystals are employed in infrared spectrophotometers. Mica crystals serve as electrical insulators. Diamonds are one of the most expensive forms (**allotropes**) of carbon. Allotropes are different forms of the same element in the same physical state. The other allotropes of carbon are graphite and the previously mentioned buckyball. Oxygen gas (O_2) and ozone (O_3) are allotropes. They both exist as gases (same physical state) and they are both composed only of the element oxygen. Ozone is a very important molecule for our existence. In the upper atmosphere it protects our planet from incoming UV radiation from the sun. As the ozone hole grows, more UV radiation is allowed to enter our atmosphere, and exposure may cause some people to develop skin cancer. However, finding O_3 in the atmosphere we normally live in is a bad thing. At these lower levels, ozone is considered to be a pollutant. Any substance in the wrong place or in the wrong concentration can be considered to be a pollutant.

Crystals grow by the addition of molecules to the outer surface of a nucleating center. The molecules must be of the same type so that they can accommodate themselves into the orderly arrangement possessed by the growing crystal. The solution in which the suspended crystal grows provides the molecules with the freedom to move about, which aids in the growth process. All crystals are solids, but the reverse is not true. For example, glass is an **amorphous** solid (particles having no orderly arrangement) of very high **viscosity.** Sometimes glass is referred to as a **liquid crystal.** One way to differentiate between a crystal and a piece of glass is to crush it. The crystal will **cleave** on predetermined faces at definite angles, but glass will fracture with no definite angles due to its curved surfaces and amorphous nature.

All crystals of one substance are alike (i.e., they have the same **intensive** properties: density, refractive index, face angles), although their **extensive** properties may vary (size, mass). Some characteristics of a crystal are a well-defined melting point (if pure), flat faces that meet at definite angles, and bonding that determines the shape and properties of the specific crystal. Crystals can be salts, nonmetallic (e.g., diamond and graphite), metallic, or **macromolecular** (e.g., silicon carbide). They are composed of **unit cells** that are the simplest repeating unit in a crystal. Unit cells are rigid and have a three-dimensional shape. **Smectic** crystals retain order in two dimensions, and **nematic** crystals retain order in three dimensions. Structures are determined by X-rays and electron defraction patterns. A **mesomorphic** crystalline structure is a crystal that exists between a solid and a liquid. A **polymorphic** crystal is one that has many shapes, and **isomorphic** crystals have the same shape. A **quasicrystal** never has a repetitive pattern. These crystals are formed by a small group of atoms forming patterns that are repeated elsewhere, but not at equal intervals. Instead, the groups are spaced in a complex manner known as **quasiperiodic** (cannot always predict where one atom will be in relation to another). Some authors suggest that these may exist in nature (e.g., aluminum and magnesium alloys may be created like this).

INVESTIGATION

Part One: Polyhedra

Materials

Platonic Nets Worksheet (Figure 13.1)

toothpicks

miniature marshmallows

construction paper in several colors

scissors

tape

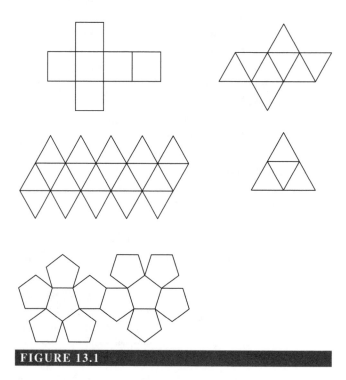

FIGURE 13.1

Exercise 1.   Each student will cut out the Platonic Nets, fold, and then tape them to form the solids.

Exercise 2.   Each student will make the Platonic Solids by using toothpicks for the edges and miniature marshmallows for the vertices.

Exercise 3

1. Complete the following table by counting the number of vertices, faces and edges.

Polyhedron	Vertices (V)	Faces (F)	Edges (E)
Tetrahedron			
Cube			
Octahedron			
Dodecahedron			
Isosahedron			

2. Develop a formula for the relationship between the number of vertices, faces and edges of the polyhedra above.

3. The formula was first discovered by René Descartes (1596–1650), a French mathematician and philosopher, then rediscovered by Swiss mathematician Leonhard Euler (1707–1783) and is named Euler's formula. Draw a prism and a pyramid below then determine whether the formula will work for these polyhedra.

4. Does the formula generalize to any polyhedron?

Exercise 4.   In science, another important discovery was made regarding polyhedra. Buckyballs are truncated icosahedron. Now, build your own buckyball.

1. Cut out 20 hexagons from one color and 12 pentagons from another color. Tape them together like the Buckyball net in Figure 13.2, then fold to form a polyhedron.
2. Determine whether Euler's formula works for the buckyball.

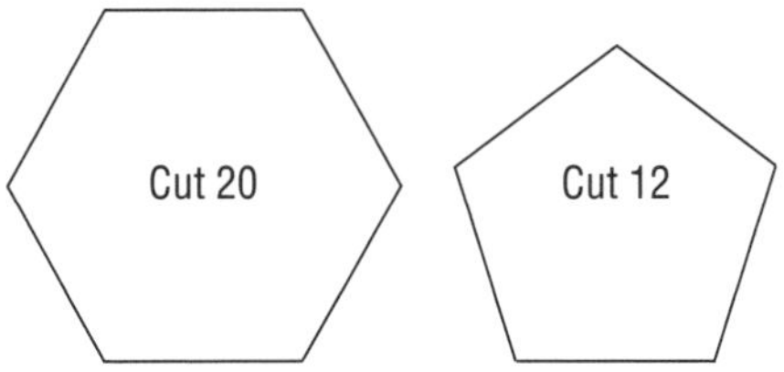

Cut 20

Cut 12

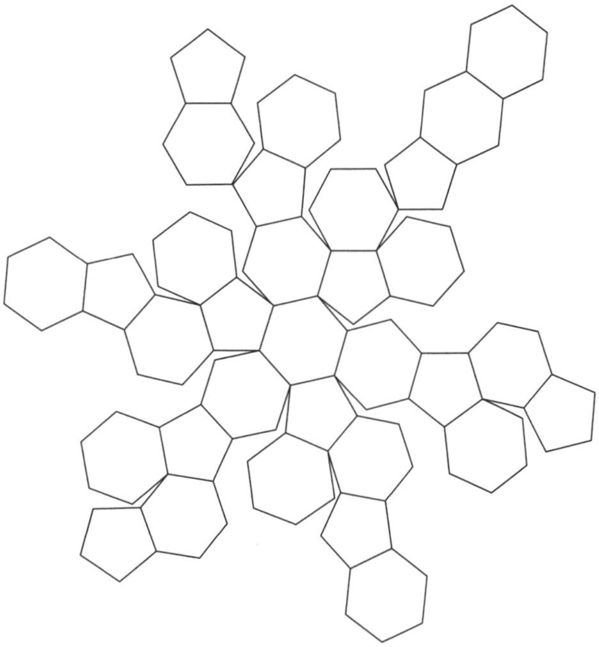

FIGURE 13.2

Exercise 5

1. Use Table 13.1 (p. 156) to make the seven crystal systems.
2. Cut out the following and use different colors.

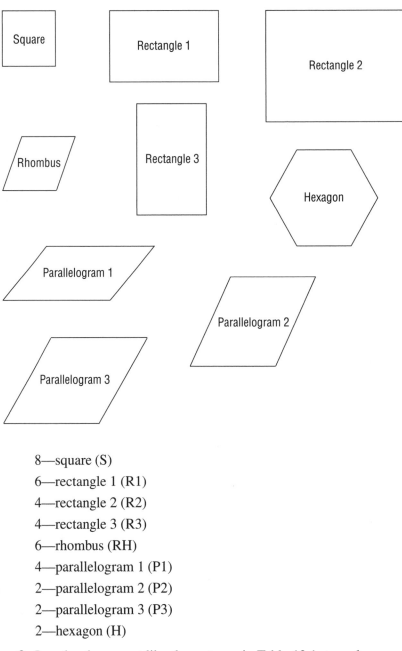

8—square (S)
6—rectangle 1 (R1)
4—rectangle 2 (R2)
4—rectangle 3 (R3)
6—rhombus (RH)
4—parallelogram 1 (P1)
2—parallelogram 2 (P2)
2—parallelogram 3 (P3)
2—hexagon (H)

3. Lay the shapes out like the patterns in Table 13.1, tape them, and then fold to make polyhedra. If the pattern has an "F," then flip the shape.
4. Verify Euler's formula for each of the seven crystal systems.

Part Two: Growing Crystals

Many crystals, quartz crystals and diamonds among them, can be grown in the laboratory, but most crystals grown in the laboratory are ionic compounds. In this investigation, you will make an attempt to grow crystals of different kinds, for example, potassium aluminum sulfate dodecahydrate (alum), "chrome alum", or one of many others that can be found in Table 13.2. You are not limited to these examples; many others are possible. Just go to the library and find your own. (The geology section of the library is a good place to start.) *The more background work you do, the better your crystal.*

It is important to keep notes on the growth of your crystal. For example, you tried something and it did or did not work, you modified the published recipe, how the crystal changed over time, appropriate information on solubility, and the function of temperature are all aspects of crystal growing that are important. Your notes will give you an insight to growing crystals that might not have surfaced if you could not refer back to them. Another good practice is to record the characteristics of your crystal (e.g., color, weight, size, and shape) each time you transfer it to a new solution.

Methods. The most effective general methods of growing crystals involve growth from a solution **saturated** with a salt at a temperature above room temperature that is allowed to cool. Crystal growth occurs either during the cooling process or at room temperature by evaporation of the solution. In either case a suitable **seed crystal** is suspended in the saturated solution and allowed to grow over a period of time.

Suitable seed crystals (1–3 mm) are obtained by preparing a saturated solution (about 200 mL) at room temperature. Next an additional amount (about equal to the amount of seed crystals hoped for) of salt is added to the

TABLE 13.2 Examples of Large Single Crystals

CRYSTAL SHAPE	CHEMICAL FORMULA	COMMENTS
Cubic	$KAl(SO_4)_2 \cdot 12H_2O$	white (colorless); octahedral crystals
	$KCr(SO_4)_2 \cdot 12H_2O$	vary Cr^{3+}/Al^{3+} ratio to give light or dark shades of purple
	$NaBrO_3$	white; tetrahedral crystals
	$NaClO_3$	white; cubic crystals; tetrahedral with added borax
	$NaCl$	white; traces of Pb^{2+} or Co^{2+} give cubic crystals
Tetragonal	$NiSO_4 \cdot 6H_2O$	green; crystals will deteriorate if not kept in a sealed bottle
Orthorhombic	$KMnO_4$	dark purple; needles
	K_2SO_4	white
	$Na_2Fe(CN)_4NO \cdot 2H_2O$	dark red-orange
Monoclinic	$Ni(NH_4)_2(SO_4)_2 \cdot 6H_2O$	green
	$K_3Fe(CN)_6$	red
Triclinic	$CuSO_4 \cdot 5H_2O$	blue; crystals will deteriorate if not kept in a sealed bottle
Hexagonal	$NaNO_3$	white; crystal exhibits double refraction

solution and heated (about 10 to 20 °C above room temperature is a good starting point) until complete **dissolution** is observed. The beaker is then covered with a watch glass and allowed to stand until crystallization is complete. Dissolution is not an immediate process; you must allow enough time for saturation to occur.

Another method for preparing the saturated solution is to add the salt slowly, with stirring, at the elevated temperature until there is a slight excess that will not dissolve. The temperature is then slowly increased until all the salt dissolves. Next remove the solution from the heat and allow it to cool slowly. When the first crystals are observed forming on the bottom of the beaker, select the best one and introduce it as the seed crystal. Place the seed crystal in the middle of approximately 300 mL of the saturated solution. Suspend a glass rod or piece of copper wire across the top of the beaker, tie a piece of fishing line to the rod or wire, and super-glue (using epoxy glue) the seed crystal onto the other end of the line. (The copper wire will allow for easy height adjustment of the crystal in solution; the crystal must not be too close to the top or bottom of the solution.) You may also wish to spread stopcock grease on the unsubmerged part of the fishing line to deter growth at this point.

Set aside the uncovered beaker (or covered with a paper towel with holes) in a place of constant temperature. A refrigerator set to –15 °C is an excellent source of constant temperature, but only place the growing chamber in the refrigerator after the solution has reached room temperature. (Some crystals grow best in a cool water bath.) To increase the size of the crystal, gradually lower the temperature of the refrigerator over the span of a number of days, and also transfer the crystal occasionally to a new saturated solution prepared like the one above. Do not allow the crystal to dry during the transfer process or subsequent growth will usually be unsatisfactory. When an adequate crystal has been obtained, it can be dried, weighed, measured, and placed in a sealed bottle. Some crystals can be coated with a spray-on polyurethane or similar product to increase their durability.

Regardless of what crystal you choose to grow, either one listed below or one that you found on your own, make sure to have a "recipe" and procedure before you start your work. **Your crystal recipes must be approved before you begin.** Also, at the end of this process, you may wish to take one of the smallest crystals and look at it under a light or polarized microscope.

How to Grow an Alum Crystal. Weigh at least 10 grams of alum, $KAl(SO_4)_2 \cdot 12H_2O$. Place it into a 250-mL beaker. For each gram of alum in the beaker add 7 mL of water. Heat to 50–60 °C and stir until the solution becomes clear. If the solution refuses to become clear, let it stand for a few minutes and then carefully decant off the clear solution. Tie a piece of fishing line to a glass rod or copper wire so that when suspended in the solution, the line will extend no more than one centimeter below the surface of the solution. Smear stopcock grease on the part of the line that will be above the solution to keep the solution from creeping up the line. Place the glass rod or copper wire on top of the beaker, cover with a paper towel held in place by a rubber band, punch a few holes (5 or 6) with a pencil into the towel, and keep the beaker in a designated storage place. Be certain that your name and the type of crystals you are growing appear on the beaker.

By the time you return for your next laboratory session, crystals should have already begun to grow. Look at what has formed and carefully brush off all but the best. If no crystals have grown, decant the liquid from the crystal or crystals at the bottom of the beaker into another beaker. Select a good seed (one that shows good faces) and super-glue this crystal onto the fishing line. Suspend the crystal in a freshly prepared solution of 10 grams of alum in 70 mL of water as described previously. This solution must be allowed to cool to room temperature before the crystal is suspended. If the solution has not been allowed to cool enough, it will not be saturated. It will start to dissolve the seed crystal and the seed crystal may slip off the line.

Repeat this procedure every laboratory session. Each time weigh your crystal and describe its appearance (color, size, weight, shape) in your notebook. At the end of the semester, you may keep your crystal. To preserve it and avoid its conversion to a white powder (by loss of water) cover it with a clear plastic spray.

How to Grow a Chrome Alum Crystal. Substitute a growing solution of chrom alum, $KCr(SO_4)_2 \cdot 12H_2O$, for the second alum growing solution. Prepare your seed crystal as described previously. Then prepare an alum solution as described, using 8 g of alum and 56 mL of H_2O. The color of this solution will be a dark blue-green. Pour this solution into the growing solution of ordinary alum slowly, while holding the solution up to the light. Stop adding the chrom alum when you can just still see through the solution. Suspend your seed crystal in the solution as before. For subsequent growing solutions use ordinary alum solutions.

CHAPTER FOURTEEN

Culminating Activities

This chapter is a collection of four activities that can be used for possible alternative assessment activities. The activities focus on upper-elementary, middle school, and high school levels supporting the concepts learned in previous chapters of the book. The first is a scavenger hunt, the second is a toy project, the third is a misconception "poster" presentation, and the fourth is a "magic of numbers" project for you to make and keep for your own use.

PART ONE: SCAVENGER HUNT

Throughout this book, you have been introduced to a variety of mathematical and scientific ideas. You have done extensive laboratory investigations and put much time and effort into learning. This activity is intended to be a fun activity to tie together many of the things that you have already seen in the book.

For this activity, you will take pictures of the following items. You may take these pictures with a digital camera, Polaroid, or regular camera. In any event, you should display each photo on its own sheet of paper with a description of where you found the item and why you believe it meets the criteria listed.

You are to turn in 25 pictures for this assignment. You may not take a picture of one object more than once (even if you find it in more than one place). You may have to go back to a previous chapter to recall a certain topic or research it elsewhere. Good luck and have fun!

Find and photograph the following items:

1. tree bark spirals
2. one sidewalk tessellation
3. the crystal you grew
4. a pattern of your choice that occurs in nature
5. a ramp and specify the angle of elevation
6. a substance with pH greater than 7.0
7. a substance containing an atom with 26 protons
8. something in harmonic motion
9. something containing an electromagnet
10. three simple machines in one picture
11. a picture or photocopy of a female physicist
12. an irregular polyhedron

13. an object that is accelerating
14. an item with potential energy
15. a paper with your normal body temperature written in °F, °C, and K
16. an inert gas
17. a simple compound whose flame test emits wavelengths in the yellow region of the spectrum
18–19. picture of someone with detached earlobes and another with attached earlobes (make sure to obtain permission!)
20–22. three examples of the practical use of the standard measurements in the USA
23–25. television ads that center on the use of physics, chemistry, and biology

PART TWO: TOY PRESENTATION

This project is a non-paper-and-pencil ORIGINAL activity appropriate for the grade you teach, would like to teach, or are currently in. The project is to be a student led demonstration using a toy. The toy cannot be a commercially manufactured educational toy. Examples of appropriate toys are yo-yo, ball, bubbles, etc. You must get prior approval from the instructor for your choice of toy. Original activity sheets appropriate for collecting data are required. The presentation must include the use of mathematics, science, and technology, and you must be very specific as to the inclusion of each of the three subject areas. You must present sample data and analysis. Supporting references are strongly suggested and the appropriate mathematics and science standards must be included.

PART THREE: MISCONCEPTION PRESENTATION

This presentation will be presented in a "poster" format. It must center on a documented misconception (documentation in educational research literature is required!) in mathematics, science, or technology. You must identify the specific misconception, and you must present a method to help students overcome the chosen misconception. Also required is a survey of at least 30 individuals as to their knowledge involving the concept. You must statistically evaluate your sample's responses and report the results using appropriate statistical measures. Higher project evaluations will be given to those who develop corrective measures that integrate mathematics, science, and technology. A written report (maximum of five typed pages, double spaced, 10–12 point font) with supporting research literature evaluated (at least three references), the correct explanation for your chosen misconception, and a written description of the appropriate corrective measure(s) to be taken are required. You will also present a poster to the class that includes the misconception question studied and the reason(s) you chose this particular misconception. Statistical results of your sample's evaluated data (pre-test is a must and a post-test after intervention is optional), corrective measures undertaken to aid student's knowledge (integration is important), and a conclusion to your study is required. Posters should be no larger than a tri-fold board and professionally done.

PART FOUR: MAGIC OF NUMBERS

At a conference for chemical educators in Texas attended in the summer of 2001, one of the presenters, Norma Ashburn, a retired chemistry teacher from South Carolina, shared a "magic" trick. She presented the trick in terms of chemistry, but we will first start it by using numbers.

Preparation

Make four large flash cards (split a piece of poster board into four quadrants) to look as these below.

Card 1			Card 2			Card 3			Card 4	
1	3		2	14		4	7		8	15
5	13		15	7		6	15		13	14
15	9		11	10		12	13		11	10
11	7		3	6		14	5		12	9

Card 1   **Card 2**   **Card 3**   **Card 4**

Now, ask your audience to pick a number on one card. Go through the series of cards above, in any order, and ask each time, "Is your number on this card?" If it is then add the number(s) of the "Yes" cards that appear in the upper left hand corner of each card. The sum should be the number chosen!

Example

The unknowing participant chooses the number, 11. Starting with Card 1, ask if the number is on that card. In the case of 11, the number 11 appears on Cards 1, 2, and 4. The sum of the top left-hand numbers of Cards 1, 2, and 4 (i.e., 1 + 2 + 8) is 11. The number 11 does not appear on Card 3, so in this case 4 is not part of the sum.

The same scenario can be used to magically identify an element from the periodic table. Assume that the numbers above are atomic numbers (the number of protons of a given element that, if known, will identify the element in question). In the place of each number, substitute the element's symbol for that atomic number (see the four cards below.) Now complete the same situation as above, but instead ask your participant to choose any element found on any card.

H	Li
B	Al
P	F
Na	N

Card 1

He	Si
P	N
Na	Ne
Li	C

Card 2

Be	N
C	P
Mg	Al
Si	B

Card 3

O	P
Al	Si
Na	Ne
Mg	F

Card 4

Example

The unsuspecting participant this time chooses the symbol, Mg for magnesium. Mg appears on Cards 3 and 4. The symbol in the top left-hand corner of Card 3 is Be (atomic number = 4) and O (atomic number = 8) is in the top left-hand corner of Card 4. The sum of 8 + 4 = 12, the atomic number of magnesium. (Of course, to play the "element" game, one must have memorized the atomic numbers for the first 15 elements! Or have a periodic table available.)

Who discovered that with the numbers 1, 2, 4 and 8 one can find sums that total 1 through 15, inclusively, we do not know, but the human ability to find patterns of nature is amazing! Finding patterns, repeating an experiment and obtaining the same result, and validating the results of a scientific experiment by carefully controlled mathematical variables combine to add to what we call *objective truth* and consequently broaden our knowledge base.